W9-AVQ-683

The Land and People of
SYRIA

SYRIA, the western end of the Mesopotamian Fertile Crescent, shared the history of the empires of the ancient world. The land was invaded by Hittites and Phoenicians, crossed by Alexander the Great, annexed by Rome. Then came the Turks, the Crusaders, and others, including the French, who held it in mandate after World War I. Syria became independent in 1946. In recent years Syria broke away from the other Arab states, and the government has undergone many changes, some of them violent. Paul W. Copeland has revised his survey of this volatile nation to include an account of recent developments in Syrian politics and in Syria's relationship with the nations of the Middle East and the West.

PORTRAITS OF THE NATIONS SERIES

The Land and People of
SYRIA

by Paul W. Copeland

PORTRAITS OF THE NATIONS SERIES

J. B. LIPPINCOTT COMPANY
Philadelphia   New York

Copyright © 1964 by Paul W. Copeland

Printed in the United States of America

Revised 1972

Map by Donald T. Pitcher

To MARY DEMING PENROSE COPELAND

Best of companions in life's adventures.

U. S. Library of Congress Cataloging in Publication Data

Copeland, Paul W
  The land and people of Syria.

  (Portraits of the nations series)
  SUMMARY: An introduction to the people, customs, history, religion, and geography of the ancient Arab country that became a new republic in 1946.

  1. Syria—Juvenile literature. [1. Syria] I. Title.
DS93.C6   1972   915.691   77-37732
ISBN-0-397-31537-6 TSE ED

The author wishes to thank the Arab Information Center for the photographs on pages 13, 27, 39, 51, 68, 72, 87, 89, 92, 104, 133, 136, 139, 147, 149, 151, 153, A. Shahinian for the photographs on pages 12, 69, 95, The National Museum of Aleppo for the photograph on page 55, and Frances Copeland Stickles for the photograph on page 123.
  All other photographs are the property of the author.

CONTENTS

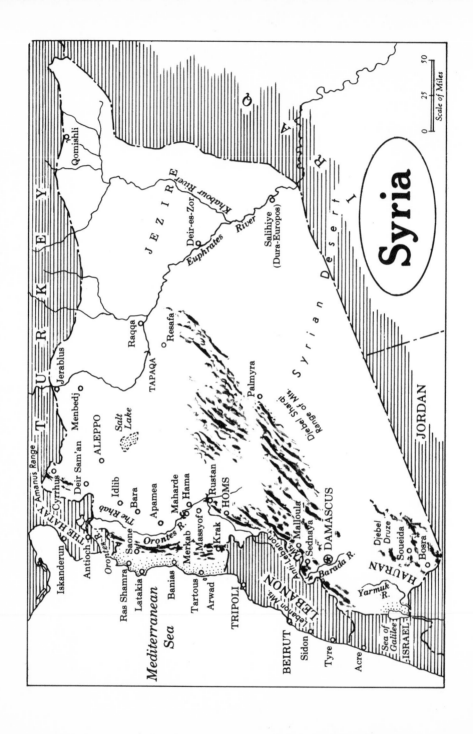

The Land and People of
SYRIA

CHAPTER ONE

Meet Syria

SYRIA, an independent self-governing country only since 1945, is an Arab state covering almost 72,500 square miles. This is an area much smaller than her neighbors Turkey, Iraq, and tremendous Saudi Arabia. It has a population of over four and a half million persons, of whom about eighty-five per cent are Muslims. Syria lies at the eastern end of the Mediterranean Sea, sharing the coastline with Lebanon, Israel, and Turkey. It is a part of the area formerly called the Near East, but since the Second World War referred to as the Middle East. This includes the countries from the eastern Mediterranean to the borders of India. On the map Syria looks like a crudely drawn diamond.

It is a forbidding land at first glance, a land of barren hills and vast deserts. But it is a land of great beauty once you get to know its many moods. In the spring the bare hills bloom with carpets of wild flowers in a profusion of colors. Every season has its distinctive charm as sunlight and shadow play like a color wheel over the red-brown hills and valleys.

Syria is bordered on the north by Turkey; on the east and southeast by Iraq; on the southwest by Jordan. On the west Syria is shut off from the seacoast by a small bit of Israel from Lake Tiberias north to the Lebanon border. North of this, Lebanon keeps Syria from the sea until its two mountain ranges, the Lebanon and Anti-Lebanon, join in a heap of lower hills called the Alawi Mountains. Through these hills Syria breaks free to the sea. The modern port of Latakia is the only large city on the eighty-five miles of coastline.

Syria again retreats from the sea behind the Turkish province of Hatay. This rich province belonged to Syria until 1939 when the French, governing Syria under a League-of-Nations mandate, gave the Hatay to Turkey as a bribe to keep her from siding with Germany in the Second World War. Turkey took the province, including the fine port of Iskanderun, or Alexandretta, and remained neutral. The Syrians have never forgotten nor forgiven this betrayal.

The hills of Northern Syria have lost their soil to the field below.

Modern Syria is at least two-thirds desert. In ancient times much of the northern desert was watered by a complex of canals leading from the Euphrates River and was rich in orchards and gardens. In Roman times Syria was considered the richest, fairest province of the Empire. But time and destructive raids of the Persians in the early seventh century and the Mongol hordes in the fourteenth and early fifteenth centuries wrecked the irrigation systems. Now every effort is being made to trace and reopen the canals. However, the barren eroded hills can never be reterraced for the earth has been washed away into the narrow valleys.

The most fertile area lies along the western border, nestled against the Anti-Lebanon Mountains. Springs and short rivers irrigate a strip of land, some thirty miles wide and 330 miles long, lying between the mountains and the desert. It is this fertile strip that supports the bulk of the population. Here you find the cities of Damascus, Homs, Hama, and Aleppo. Here also are the farms of wheat, barley, cotton, melons, and sugar beets. Vineyards climb the mountain slopes. Great orchards of olives, figs, apricots, pomegranates, pistachios, and almonds give color and shade to the otherwise bare landscape.

These same mountains that give life to this fertile strip rob most of the rest of Syria of the rain clouds from the sea. What rain that gets past the mountains falls during the winter months of December to March. When it does rain it pours in torrents that cut gullies in the bare hills and strew the roads with boulders. Ordinary highway drains would choke up, so the gullies or *wadis,* as they are called, are paved with an apron of concrete to carry storm water over the road. The storms go as quickly as they come and in between them the sun shines in a cold pale blue sky.

Water is the key to Syria's survival. A few rivers save part of the land and support farming. The Orontes River flowing northward from Lebanon provides water for irrigation around Homs and Hama. Here the sugar beet is supplanting the less profitable sugar cane. The

Washed wheat is spread to dry before storing for the winter.

Orontes great marshes, called the Rhab, to the north and west of Hama, are being drained to provide more precious farm land. The river then wanders north into Turkey. Along the border tobacco, cotton, and rice are the major crops.

This plain beside the mountains is also watered from a few springs in the mountains and from wells. Village wells, once from sixteen to twenty feet deep, are having to be drilled deeper and deeper. The water level of the whole Arabian peninsula is dropping alarmingly. It is feared that the water, accumulated through millions of years of seepage, is rapidly being exhausted by the use of power-driven pumps.

The Euphrates is the only large river in Syria. It originates in Turkey and cuts diagonally across the northeast corner of the country. This large triangle of land, called the Jezire, is also watered by the Khabour River and lesser tributaries. The area supports large ranches growing wheat and cotton. Wheat is the staple food of the country; it used to be the major crop. In recent years cotton has taken the lead as the most valuable crop.

South of the Euphrates is now largely desert with the exception of the oasis of Palmyra east of Homs. There springs of water, sulfurous but drinkable, support large groves of date palms. Agriculture improves in the southwest corner of the country where the Yarmuk River irrigates the plain spoken of as the Hauran.

The winter is cold, often with snow on the hills. The stone buildings with their tile floors can get painfully cold in spite of oil stoves or charcoal braziers in every room. Schoolboys and girls wear their overcoats, mittens, and caps in the classroom; some even carry pillows to protect themselves from the cold chairs.

On the other hand, spring is so short as to pass almost unnoticed.

A modern irrigation dam near Homs.

The long summer from May to mid-October is hot with temperatures well above a hundred degrees. By the first of May it is so hot that the schools go on a summer schedule, starting classes at six-thirty in the morning and closing at noon. After lunch everyone takes a long siesta. Then about four o'clock the shops reopen and the people stroll along the streets or shop during the short twilight.

Spring, although short, provides a glorious display of wild flowers in the otherwise bare fields: tiny star flowers in yellow, pink, and white; poppies, crocus, grape hyacinths, and many varieties of ranunculus. Indeed, every familiar garden flower seems to have its smaller, wild original here. They bloom alongside the roads and cover the fields like carpets, even where the ground is incredibly rocky.

The native black iris, taken to Europe by the Crusaders, is the parent of the hundreds of varieties that adorn western gardens today. The Arabs call it the "flower of death" and plant it only on graves. Another flower associated with death is the asphodel. It blooms in the fields in great profusion most of the summer. A tall stalk, growing out of a cluster of leaves like a foxglove, bears a cluster of small, ash-pink flowers. They are so neutral in color, it is easy to see why the ancient Greeks considered the asphodel the flower of the Elysian fields where the shades of the departed dead roamed in bleak loneliness.

The flowered carpets on hill and valley fade all too soon under the hot summer sun. But trees, given a bit of water, do surprisingly well. Along the streams are willows, oleanders, and cottonwoods. Farmers in the north are now planting cottonwoods along the irrigation ditches both as a windbreak and as a marketable timber crop. In five years they have trees large enough to be used as scaffolding; in seven years, strong enough to be sold as ceiling rafters. Oak and pine trees cluster in the mountain valleys but most of the timber of ancient days is gone. During the First World War the Turks cut what was left to keep their railroads operating. Reforestation is defeated by the goats which eat the seedlings. Every *mahaffasite,* or province, is expected to maintain a tree farm, but the program is making slow headway against the ravages of the goats.

In the towns and cities trees are cultivated for their shade and fragrance. The golden jasmine, blue jacaranda, the orange-red flame tree, pale blue mimosa, and white locust blossoms lend perfume to the air as well as beauty to the streets. Junipers make a dark contrast to the white walls of buildings, and the cypress grows tall like the nearby slender minarets of the mosques. Roses bloom all summer long in the private gardens and courtyards. Lemon trees, planted outside the bedroom windows, are supposed to keep the flies away, but they do a very poor job of it.

After the heavy spring rains, truffles literally pop out of the desert ground. You scan the surface for a small mound wrinkled with cracks. It is unnecessary to train dogs or pigs to hunt for them, as farmers do in France. A stick will poke out the delicious roots shaped like small turnips. Considered a luxury in Europe, in Syria they are called "the poor man's potatoes."

In the animal world, the native Syrian ass is a light grey, slender-boned, graceful cousin to the more familiar donkey. Both can carry incredible loads, usually with patient resignation. When they do protest, however, it is with an ear-splitting braying to be heard for blocks. The donkey is the poor man's auto. Found everywhere in town and countryside, his tremendous loads of brush or bags of chaff completely hide him, and the load often appears to be moving along on some mysterious power of its own.

Goats are a common source of income, whether they be two or three or herds numbering hundreds. They graze on the scanty grass as long as it lasts; then they must move on to find new pastures or to be fed such things as watermelons. In the cities the goats, driven by a herder, are the ambling garbage collectors. The garbage is put in holes in the parking strips and every evening the goats are driven over a regular route through the streets. They clean up everything but the few tin cans. These are carefully collected by the goatherd,

The load is bigger than the donkey.

who sells them to the tinsmiths to be made into an unbelievable variety of utensils.

Sheep are the major source of meat, but, like the goats, give milk and wool as well. They can also survive on a very little pasturage. Most sheep are of the Asian, or fat-tail breed. The tail is shaped like that of a beaver and, when rendered, provides a popular cooking oil. In the mountain villages with practically no pasturage, it is the practice to tie a sheep and the youngest member of the family together on the flat roof. The child stuffs the sheep with leaves or grass until the tail becomes so fat, weighing up to fifty pounds, that the sheep cannot move. Then a wooden ski or a little axle with wooden wheels is attached to the tail so the sheep can move about.

The Syrian lion in olden times roamed the desert in large numbers. Hunting him was the "sport of kings," as many ancient sculptures show. They have been gone for less than a century. Until the late nineteenth century it was still considered a test of manhood for men of the upper Euphrates area to challenge a lion in single combat. Of course the whole village would go along to watch.

It was customary for the challenger to arm himself with a short sword and to wrap his left arm with yards of goat yarn. Then he stood before the lion's den and hurled insults on the lion and on all its ancestors as only an Arab can. The villagers stayed discreetly at a distance. When the lion charged, the trick was to thrust the left arm into the lion's open mouth. As the lion instinctively raised his paws to hold the mouthful more firmly, the hunter would hamstring the beast and stab it to death. A clever trick if you can do it.

The gazelle, a beautiful small antelope about thirty inches high, also lives in the desert. The Bedouins hunt them with trained falcons, but they are also chased by hunters in jeeps. This modern form of hunting is not as unfair to the gazelle as it sounds, for the bouncing jeep often spills the hunters and they come home with broken bones instead of game. Jackals still howl and prowl, attacking the unwary gazelle but living largely on the desert hares. Occasionally of an evening you can see the small red desert fox flashing across the road.

The camel, major beast of burden, was introduced from Asia about 1100 B.C. by the Midianites. The Bedouins raise both the work camel and the racing camel. For the most part camels are evil-tempered brutes, ready to kick or to spit their horrible smelling cud at you. They are arrogant, will not make way for anyone, and are very particular about the weight of the load they will consent to carry. However, they are an ideal form of transportation in a desert land, for their padlike feet make perfect sand-shoes and they can go several days without water. Camels, even more than goats or sheep, justify their pampered existence. Besides providing an ideal means of desert transportation, camels also supply meat, milk, and wool. The skin is used for bags and shoes, and the wool makes the thick felt of Bedouin tents and the best quality of cloth for *abbas,* or square-cut cloaks worn indoors or out.

The Arab horse, rather small, slender, and proud of bearing, is the ancestor of most Western race horses today. The horse and the chariot were introduced into Syria and Egypt about the eighteenth century B.C. by the Hyksos, a mixed people from the north who were referred to on Egyptian records as "the shepherd people." Breeding Arab horses has been intensified in recent years due to a new appreciation of their special qualities as race horses. The region of Hama and the surrounding Bedouin camps is the center for breeding horses. Many Bedouin tribes take pride in their horses and can recite from memory the pedigrees that go back hundreds of years.

Bird life is surprisingly extensive. Huge eagles of six-foot wing spread cruise over the desert along with buzzards twice the size of turkeys. Falcons and hawks soar lazily in the sky. Grey crows with black caps and wing patches are as big as gulls. They walk around tamely like chickens picking up insects. Golden canaries, finches, sparrows, swallows, and doves, to name but a few of the familiar birds, move about in large flocks. Doves are raised in large numbers for food and for fertilizer. Most villages have a square dovecot, two stories high, looming above the houses.

Along the Orontes River, marshes of the Rhab and the Euphrates River are ducks, plover, and reed birds of all kinds. Partridges are hunted on the desert. In the spring huge flights of storks appear on their migration from Africa to southern Turkey, where they build their large untidy nests. Quite tame, they stand on one leg by the roadside and view the passing traffic with condescending indifference.

Probably the most unusual and certainly the most beautiful bird is a cinnamon-colored one the size of a large pigeon. Bold black and white stripes, like a sergeant's chevrons, blaze on wings and back. It has a long curved bill and on its head a black-tipped crest that can open and shut like a fan. It is the hoopoe, famed for its cry, which in Arabic means "up, up."

Dogs and cats are everywhere. Most are wild and travel in hungry, vicious packs. The village dogs are as large and fierce as the wolves from which they are descended. Both animals are tolerated by the Arabs but not petted or loved. Tolerance depends on their usefulness in catching destructive rodents. They must fend for themselves, for no villager has any food to spare for them.

As far as Arab dogs are concerned, the only breed given exceptional care is the saluki. This sleek, swift dog is raised by the Bedouins and is used to hunt the smaller game of the desert. It is the pampered pet of the whole camp and is even permitted inside the black tents.

In Aleppo, amazingly, there is an endowed Cat Mosque, Madrasah Othmaniyyah, complete with staff, where cats are fed daily. It is a weird sight at dusk to see scores of mangy, scrawny cats running toward the mosque for their dinner.

The golden hamster is the smallest but most lovable of Syria's strange animals. All the hamsters in the Western world are descendants of a mother hamster and her twelve little ones who were dug out of their burrow near Aleppo only a few years ago. As you know, they make wonderful pets and are invaluable in scientific research.

No physical description of Syria would be complete without mentioning the hundreds of flat-topped mounds that dot the lands around the desert. They are known by the Arabic name *tell,* meaning an artificial man-made mound. A tell is the accumulation of a number of villages or cities each built on the debris of an earlier settlement. In Syria these mud-brick villages rise about five inches a century. War, pestilence, or famine may wipe out a village. The mud-brick houses collapse under the heavy winter rains. Later, other people come by, level off the debris, and build again on the same site, for

The modern village of Tell T'Arif is gradually devouring an ancient tell.

it was originally chosen for some advantage, a good spring, an easily defended hill, a river ford, or a convenient stop on a caravan route. Consequently people return and build again and again on the same spot until the site rises higher and higher to become a hill with a distinctive flat top.

Archeologists, slicing through a tell as you might through a layer cake, find layers of walls and floors, discarded pots, and broken tools, each layer older than the one on top of it. The story, told in reverse of their digging, gives the life history of its many peoples. Hundreds of these tells rise from the Syrian plain, mute but arresting evidence of how long men have been living and dying in this ancient land.

CHAPTER TWO

Strange Customs, Friendly People

ON A first visit to Syria one is struck by the great volume of noise: people shouting, radios blaring, taxis honking, all producing a continuous hubbub. This crescendo of sound further confuses the visitor when the shouting is all in Arabic or Armenian.

Anthropologists, who study the behavior of man, tell us that talking and singing at the top of one's lungs is an inherited habit; that shouting was early man's defense against the awesome silence of the desert. If that be true the majority of Oriental peoples must have originated in the desert.

Syrians certainly love music and singing. Almost every village has a "combo" of drums, fifes, and variations of the guitar. Singing in groups is very popular and usually ends in a contest to prove which group can drown out the other. Large clay tubes pinched in at the waist with skins stretched over both ends make good bongo-type drums. The player balances the drum on one knee and taps out the rhythms with the fingers of both hands.

To most Western ears, the tunes seem monotonous, for the Arabic musical scale contains intervals less than ours and too subtle to be appreciated by the average foreigner. In both singing and playing, the louder the music the better it is.

One of the tortures of riding in a *service,* or long distance taxi, is that for hours the car radio blares at full volume. The foreigner arrives at his destination with a splitting headache while everybody else in the car had a most enjoyable trip shouting their conversation over the din.

Another surprise to the visitor is Arab family life. In Syria, as in the rest of the Middle East, the father is the arbitrary head of the family. His word is law even when the sons are grown up and married. They are expected to continue to live under the paternal roof and spending money is doled out to them by the father.

Today there is a quiet revolt stirring among the educated young men. Syria's expanding economy offers them more opportunities to get jobs as sales-representatives, insurance agents, importers, government clerks. These and other small businesses provide an economic escape from dependence on the father.

The boom in apartment building in all larger cities is said to be sparked by young couples refusing to stay under the parents' roof. They insist on striking out on their own. Such independence should build a more responsible class of citizens to help a young nation grow toward maturity.

In spite of the traditional control of the family by the father there is little of the "togetherness" so common to Western families. Seldom do the members of an Arab family sit together for meals. The servants rise early and prepare the food for the day. Members of the family eat when hunger dictates. In upper class, wealthier families, one is startled to see a huge refrigerator standing in the dining room. It has a padlock on it and the adult members of the family carry keys. The lock keeps the children and servants from taking unauthorized snacks.

Servants are in general demand. Even relatively poor families have at least one. They are usually village girls who are bound out for seven years of service. The father is paid a lump sum, sometimes less than one hundred dollars. The girl gets her bed and board and a few clothes.

Servants are often treated much like slaves and are expected to be on the job at any time of day or night. If the master brings guests home with him at one or two o'clock in the morning, the servants must prepare a dinner. They will also be expected to sweep down the stairs and wash the tile terraces by five o'clock the same morning. Like soldiers in a continual battle of work, servants catch bits of sleep when they can.

Servants are needed to do the jobs for which Western people have mechanical equipment and labor-saving devices. In even a modern apartment house the kitchen is equipped with a cold-water tap, a precast concrete sink, a tile drainboard, and a drain in the middle of the tile floor. There are no cupboards for dishes, pans, and pots, no work table or built-in counters. Electric toasters, coffee-makers, and beaters are conspicuous by their absence. There is no electric or gas range.

A hot-water line can be hooked up from a tank burning *mazout* kerosene or olive-pits sold in bags. But more often all water is heated on a "primus" or "puffer," a kerosene burner that needs continual pumping to keep it going. These burners are usually placed on the floor, even for cooking food. When a charcoal brazier is used for broiling, it must be taken outside on the back balcony for fear of spreading deadly fumes inside the house.

Foreign families usually have servants trained in European cookery and household routines. In Syria, many of the menservants are Nestorians or Palestinian refugees who learned their skills while working for the British armies in the Middle East. They make wonderful servants who can be trusted to run the household, taking great pride in their reputation for honesty. They say, "We are not *jungly people*," a term picked up in India denoting a low-class unreliable people. They prefer to work only for the well-educated families living on regular schedules.

It is a surprise to find the restrictive Muslim customs surviving in large modern cities. Even in the new apartment houses designed in the latest Mediterranean style, the suites are planned with two reception rooms, one for men and one for women. One wall of the men's reception room is usually decorated with a large marble slab holding the electric fuses and meter. This is the only room a strange man from outside the family, like a meter-reader, may enter.

A Muslim may play host to foreign guests, men and women, but usually the wife does not join in the party. Afterward, she entertains the women alone in her own reception room. It is only in the well-educated and more liberal families that both husband and wife are hosts together.

This separation of the sexes goes farther. Special parks are set aside for women and children only. Here the women may chat together with their veils lifted off their faces. The motion picture theaters, and they are many and popular, hold daily matinees for women only. Muslim men go alone in the evening. Similarly one never asks a Muslim about his wife, a question such as a Westerner would use to open a friendly conversation.

On the other hand, there is great curiosity about Western ways of living. An Arab guest has no hesitation in asking questions that seem rude to the foreign host. He may roam around your living room and ask what you paid for each piece of furniture. However, there is no intention of rudeness, he is just frankly interested.

Another custom strange to Americans and Europeans is the leisurely manner in which business is transacted. Westerners used to the rush and crush of department-store sales are surprised and pleased to be greeted by the shopkeeper and engaged in a leisurely conversation while sipping coffee or tea.

Stores with fixed prices are new to the Middle East. It is considered more fun to barter. The seller names an exorbitant figure; the buyer suggests an equally ridiculous low figure. Gradually, step by step, the buyer and seller reach a price midway, and satisfactory to both.

Unfortunately the tempo of life in Syria is quickening as the country hastens to modernize, and this pleasant custom is dying out. In the larger cities more and more stores sell at fixed prices where you dash in, make your purchase, and dash out. It may be more efficient, but it is not as pleasant as the old way.

The custom of tipping varies in different countries but in Syria, asking for a tip, or *bakhshish,* has become a high art. When renting an apartment you pay a year's rent in advance. When you are ready to move in, there is a touching ceremony with your landlord—*touching* in more ways than one. The landlord makes a sentimental speech of welcome. In flowery Arabic phrases, he tells you that his house is yours, that he is your father, and that he and you are all one happy family. Then he hands you the large bunch of keys to all your doors, and you hand over the "key money" of over two or three hundred

Conservative Muslim women still wear black cloaks and veils.

dollars as bakhshish. That is the most touching part of the ceremony. When you buy any expensive item like a rug, radio, or a
piece of furniture, everyone concerned in the transaction expects a
large tip. Small sums in bakhshish go to the boy who carries your
purchases from the store to your car, to the man who dusts off your
parked car, the gardener, the watchman at the doorway, and to his
assistant who opens the door.

The day after Christmas, which corresponds to Boxing Day in
Britain, the street sweepers, garbage collectors, janitors, and many
other persons you never saw before, call for bakhshish. An extreme
example of asking for bakhshish is the device of the beggarwomen
on the streets. They dope their babies with opium so that they look
sick. The sympathy of the passer-by is aroused and he gives the
wretched mother as many coins as he can spare.

The short spring is ushered in with a number of rites peculiar
to the Syrians. There is the custom of everyone strolling around
eating long-leaved lettuce. About the time the sidewalks are littered
with wilted lettuce leaves, the tinsmiths start on their annual rounds.
Setting up shop in the street or on any vacant lot, they do a thriving
business retinning pots and pans. Servants bring copper cooking
vessels to have the tin lining renewed. The tinsmith uses a cold
solder that lasts only a year before it must be renewed again to
avoid copper poisoning. This is also the time for crews of men to go
about the city cleaning rugs. The job is usually done in the street,
adding more obstacles to traffic. Rugs are swept vigorously on both
sides and then shaken by a man holding each end. Camphor is scattered over them and they are rolled and stored away for the long
summer. Bare tiled floors are preferred for summer coolness. Donkeys loaded with rugs pass on their way to the rug mart in the *souk*
or bazaar. Many families simply rent rugs for the winter months and
return them to the dealer in the spring.

Rugs are also used to decorate the houses when an important visitor is to arrive. The family's best rugs hang from the balconies, an

The city of Homs with the Grand Mosque in the center.

improvement over bedraggled bunting. The rug is a sign of welcome, implying "My house is your house." Undoubtedly it is the origin of our custom of "rolling out the red carpet" for important visitors.

When the King of Saudi Arabia visited Syria in 1952, the city of Homs put up a magnificent display of rugs. Temporary wooden frames held them, making a wall of color along three sides of the square. An American, marveling out loud that it was safe to leave them there for days, was told by a passer-by, "Everyone knows the rugs of each family. To take one would be like stealing a branded horse in your country—and just as deadly."

Funeral customs differ from ours. Every Muslim at death must have his own grave, where his face is turned toward Mecca. As you can imagine, through the centuries the cemeteries have spread so that they cover acres and acres, and headstones are often as close together as rows of dominoes on end.

As is customary in all hot countries, death is followed by a seemingly hasty burial, preferably the same day. In Muslim countries details may vary slightly but in general the corpse is washed, the hands are arranged in an attitude of prayer, and the body is wrapped in strips of cloth like a mummy. If the family is poor or from a small village, the body will be tied to two poles to be carried to the graveyard.

The women stay at home to grieve while the men act as the bearers. The procession seems noisy and confused as male friends and strangers rush to help carry the body for a short distance, for all the bearers are believed to gain credit in heaven for their volunteer help.

In the towns and cities a casket will be borrowed from the mosque and a brief detour may be made to the mosque for prayers. A wealthy family will probably buy a new coffin and later give it to the mosque to be used by less fortunate families. At the grave the corpse is removed from the coffin and placed on its side in the grave, facing Mecca. A sheikh, or a religious teacher, instructs the spirit of the dead man in the proper answers he is to give the judgment angels awaiting him in the next world.

Usually the family receives intimate friends at home for three nights afterward, and acquaintances drop in once to pay their condolence calls. Specially trained blind sheikhs have been invited to the house to recite the whole Koran. They are fed food and sweets and are noted for the quantity they can consume in three days.

If death cannot be denied, at least minor disasters can be avoided by the color blue, a belief still common according to dictionary meanings of blue. Arab children, donkeys, and camels all wear necklaces of blue beads as a charm against evil spirits. Similarly, the herds of goats and flocks of sheep are protected by their leaders. The

Sheep follow their leader, protected by a blue head charm.

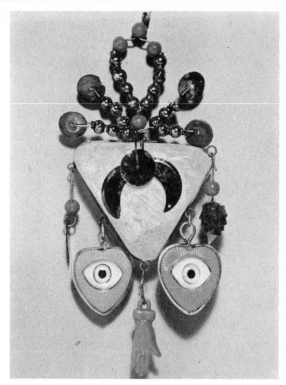

An alum charm wards off evil.

animals wear collars of blue beads or have their horns daubed with blue paint. Most village women are partial to blue dresses for the same protective reason.

Along with the color blue, the astringent salt crystals of alum have magic protective powers recognized throughout the Mediterranean area. In Syria the present-day protective charm for travelers is a decorated triangle of alum. Taxi and bus drivers hang the charms from the rear-view mirror. They are a comforting sight to the passengers, who need all the protection available against reckless drivers. The astringent alum charm is also a first-aid kit, handy to help stop bleeding in case of accidents!

The charm consists of a triangle of alum crystal supported by decorative strands of wired beads. On the alum triangle are the inverted horns of the ancient bull god of virility and two staring eyeballs of the eye goddess. From the bottom of the crystal hangs the protective hand of Fatima, Muhammed's favorite daughter. When this charm is blessed by a holy man conveniently near the taxi-stand, all contingencies and all faiths have been covered. How can one have a disaster after all that?

Crops were originally protected by "corn dollies" made from the last sheaf of wheat, oats, or barley to be harvested. This sheaf, dressed up like a doll, was carefully preserved to insure another harvest in the year to come. In many farming communities throughout Europe and England, the custom still persists in one form or another as part of the harvest frolic. In Ireland, for instance, they are called St. Brigid's Crosses.

In Syria, down through the centuries the corn dolly has moved from the field into the house to protect the family as well as the crops. The Arab village dolly is a simple stick figure of crossed stalks of wheat tied in bundles with gay yarns and banded with bright tin foil. In villages along the northern border, the crossarm acquires a thick skirt of wheat stalks that makes the dolly look much like a Scot's sporran. With the Turkomen the dolly acquires an elaborately decorated diamond-shaped body with a three- to four-foot skirt of strings of chick-peas. The pea pods, about one-half inch in diameter and the color of a peanut shell, contain a dozen little black seeds.

In times of family trouble or calamity, a pod is pinched off and the seeds are sprinkled on the fire. The pungent, aromatic smoke carries the family prayers to the protective god. Burning the seeds also provides an effective air-freshener to drive out unpleasant odors. A visitor's casual glance at the number of missing pods will give an accurate estimate of the family's fortunes of the year.

Another odd custom might be called the "sympathy strike." When any major event occurs in the Arab world, such as a shooting incident on the Turkish or Israeli borders, a massacre in Algeria, or a riot in Iraq, all students go out on strike. They parade through the streets, make speeches in front of the post office, and end up at the movies. The sympathy strikes seem to be prompted by the intense feeling of unity shared by all the Arab nations. The students, sharing this strong emotion, also share the delight all schoolboys show for an excuse to take a holiday away from the classroom.

This is only one more example of the fact that people everywhere share the same emotions. Strange customs are usually superficial, and underneath, people the world over are much alike.

CHAPTER THREE

Peoples and Faiths

THE PEOPLE of Syria have been a part of the land for so long a time it is impossible to discuss one without the other. For thousands of years they have occupied a harsh land and have adapted themselves to living on it and with it.

The people are Arabs of Semitic stock and are, for the most part, Muslims in religion and culture. On the whole, they are a small, slight-framed people with brunet complexions. They usually have black hair, strong noses, expressive dark eyes, and erect postures. Occasionally you will see a redhead, formerly considered a descendant from some Crusader. Now red hair is recognized as a definite Mediterranean strain. Of course the people are of all sizes and shapes like the rest of us, but the older merchants and the women tend to put on weight from too rich food and too little exercise. Most of the young men and young girls are quite handsome, with a uniform good looks that is particularly noticeable to Americans who are used to their wide variety of "melting-pot" faces.

In the villages the dress is much the same as that worn in Bible times. The men wear a striped cotton robe like an old-fashioned nightshirt, called a *galabyia,* over white cotton pants, both held in at the waist by a sash. Unfortunately it has become the fad to wear a European jacket over the galabyia. The men wear a head-scarf, *kaffiyah,* held firmly by a coil of weighted black cord, *agal,* over a tight skullcap. The kaffiyah is a perfect protection against desert sun and heat.

The village women wear long red pants ruffled at the ankles. Over them they put on as many gaily colored dresses as they own and cover their heads with a turban-like scarf. Their feminine beauty is often marred, at least in Western eyes, by blue tribal tattoo marks on forehead or chin. The women do most of the field work, bending from the waist with legs straight. When in the field they roll their skirts around their waists, and all you see from a distance are bodyless red pants walking around the field, a startling spectacle. Muslim village women do not wear veils over their faces. They take an active, forceful part in village affairs and manage their menfolk with the skill of wives the world over.

Most young village girls collect gold coins toward their dowry. These are sewn to a narrow cloth band and worn on the forehead. After marriage the coins represent a savings account, added to in good years and in bad times sold to carry the family through the crisis. With the disappearance of gold coinage, they are now thin imitations bought by weight in the gold shops.

In the city it is usually the workmen and male servants who cling to the old costumes of baggy black pants, *sherwal,* tapering in at the ankles, and white collarless shirts. Many of them have taken to the European jacket. The business and professional men have largely adopted European clothing. The tarboush, or red fez, required headgear under Turkish rule, is rapidly disappearing. The Muslim women of the city have generally accepted European styles of dress. The more conservative, however, still wear a voluminous black cloak and a veil, *ezar,* that covers the head and face when they leave their homes. Most of the educated young Muslim women have discarded

Young village girls dressed for a party.

the veil for dark sunglasses.

The people cannot be completely described without considering their religious beliefs. Through the centuries religions have sprouted, flourished, and withered, leaving little segments of peoples banded closely together in mutual defense of their faiths. In Europe or America two men meeting will soon ask the question, "What do you do?" or "What is your business?" In Syria, as in the rest of the Middle

East, the question is, "What is your religion?" The answer to that question identifies your social group, your status in the community, and often your political convictions. Consequently people of the same faith tend to group together, living and working in the same quarters of the city or in a village by themselves. This is all very confusing and often incomprehensible to the Western visitor. Westerners are used to accepting people without first questioning their racial backgrounds or religious beliefs. In Syria you can avoid making tactless mistakes if you can first determine a person's religion.

Most Arabs are Muslims who practice Islam, a religion founded by Muhammed in the seventh century. The Syrian Muslims are largely Sunnis. They accept the Koran as their Bible and the Sunna, the orthodox traditions about Muhammed, as their way of life. Muhammed they believe to be the chief Prophet of Allah or God.

Islam, meaning "submission to the will of God," was a way of life ideally suited to desert peoples, for it provided definite rules of good conduct, exciting opportunities for conquest and conversion, and a promise of a future life free of desert hardships. The new converts' enthusiastic acceptance and missionary zeal carried the faith west to Spain and eastward as far as the Philippines. Moreover, it spread the common language, Arabic, to a variety of peoples. The Arab love of poetry and their practice of memorizing developed a love of the language for its own musical sounds. The Koran was not put in written form until twenty years after Muhammed's death, but his words and notes, written on palm leaves and on other odd materials, had been committed to memory by his followers.

The "High" Arabic spoken by a few scholars is incomprehensible to ordinary Arabs and foreigners alike, yet the cadence and rhythm enchant the listener. No language holds a variety of peoples under its spell and awe as does Arabic.

In addition to the Sunni Muslims there are a few villages of Shi'ite Muslims in Syria. They are the second largest sect of Islam and most of them live in Iran. They consider the first three caliphs, a title meaning "successor," elected after Muhammed's death to be impostors, and believe that the line of succession should come down from Ali, Muhammed's son-in-law. Their religious beliefs and practices include parts of the ancient Persian religion of Zoroaster. Consequently there is a sharp division between the two sects, Sunni and Shi'ah, with each suspicious of the other.

Islam has five basic commands called pillars. The first is the command to believe in one God, Allah, and in Muhammed, his Prophet. The second pillar is prayer, five times daily in ritual purity, that is, after washing carefully before kneeling in prayer facing toward Mecca. In cities and towns the faithful are reminded by the call of the muezzin from the minaret or tower, close to the mosque or Islamic church. The muezzin is a trained singer who chants the call to prayer at dawn, noon, midafternoon, sunset, and dusk. The chant is beautiful to listen to in the quiet of dawn before the noises of the day begin. Unfortunately some of the big city mosques have modernized and play a record through loud-speakers. The third pillar is almsgiving to the poor, to be done personally and not through an agency. Estates left to charity go to a pious foundation called the Waqf, administered by judges called cadi. Fasting and the pilgrimage to Mecca, the last two pillars, will be described in a later chapter.

Friday noon is the time for public prayers at the mosque. Here the imam, or prayer leader, will lead the worshippers in passages from the Koran, give a short sermon, and make such announcements as are important to the congregation. Friday is not a holy day of rest as the Christian Sunday used to be, but shops are usually closed during the hour of the service. It is also a big market day when country people come to the towns to sell their wares or their produce. Government offices are usually closed for the day and it is becoming more and more common for business offices to follow their example and provide a day of rest for their employees.

Most pious Muslims carry a small prayer rug. It is designed with spaces on which to place the hands when kneeling in prayer. But the poorer suppliant, such as a laborer, can be seen to use any piece of cloth he may have. Pious Muslims do not drink alcoholic beverages because Muhammed forbade such practices. However, a native distillation from grapes or dates, called *arak,* is considered a beneficial aid to digestion.

Smoking is also frowned upon, but the hookah, or "hubble-bubble" pipe is very popular in the coffeeshops and village guest houses. Instead of fidgeting with cigarettes, the men carry a string of thirty-three beads that they constantly finger. Many Christian Arabs do the same, calling them "worry beads." To the Muslim, the thirty-three beads represent the names of Allah; to the Christian, the years of Christ's life.

The mosque may be a simple building of whitewashed mud brick, a converted Byzantine church, or a colorfully tiled jewel of Islamic architecture. There was no attempt at a standardized plan until the great architect Sinan built more than one hundred mosques and schools during the reign of Suleiman the Magnificent, caliph from 1520 to 1566. In all cases a dome identifies a mosque, with one or more minarets beside it. A courtyard in front provides a pool or basins for the ritual or purification by washing. Inside the mosque, the floor will be covered with rugs and both worshipper and visitor will take off their shoes before entering. In one wall a niche, called the *mihrab,* indicates the direction of Mecca, so that even the blind may know the direction in which to pray. There will also be a pulpit, called the *minbar,* on top of a flight of steps that is often built of beautifully inlaid woods. Here the imam will lead the reading of the Koran and will preach on Friday. To Western eyes the interior seems bare because there is no resplendent altar on which to focus one's attention.

Islam, like all other great religions, has many minor, splinter sects. One relatively small group, the Ismailis, live in the mountain villages grouped around the larger town of Massyaf. The Ismailis are a branch of the Shi'ite sect of Persia where they originated.

The Mosque of Khosrofiyyah in Aleppo, from the citadel.

In the eleventh century, a Persian named Hasan-as-Sabah founded a religious order on military lines. Members, on initiation, vowed absolute obedience to Sabah as the Grand Master. The order grew rapidly, spreading east and west. A lodge was established in Syria at Massyaf where its converts filled the big castle and the surrounding villages.

In 1162 Rashid el-Din Senan became Grand Master of Syria. He was a strange and ruthless leader whose policy of political control by assassination made him feared by Muslims and Christians alike. The Crusaders called him "Old Man of the Mountain" and paid him an annual tribute. His agents were presumed to be doped with hashish, sometimes known as kef. The drug, made from the flower of the Indian hemp, produced enticing visions of paradise. After such visions, the converts were eager to go on their murderous missions. The Ismaili called a user of hashish a *hashashi*, which has given us the word "assassin."

Today their harmless, hard-working descendants are a part of the half million or more Ismailis scattered around the world. Recently the most famous hereditary grand master was the late Aga Khan whose antics fascinated the world of international society.

These Ismaili people stay much to themselves, tending their sheep and goats and farming their rocky valleys. They are typical mountain folk, rather contemptuous of the lowlanders around them. But in spite of their sinister past history, they, like all Arabs, make any visitor welcome.

North of the Ismailis, and living in a similar jumble of hills, is another divergent sect called the Alawi or Nusayris. Their religion is thought to stem from the Phoenicians, with a few elements of the Shi'ite branch of Islam added. It certainly contains many features of pagan nature worship. They have no organized churches or mosques but revere saints' tombs and such spots as springs, holy trees, and sacred hilltops. They number about 275,000, earning a meager living grazing sheep, goats, and cattle. In the summer they move on to a coastal plain around Latakia, live in crude reed houses shaped like the Quonset huts of World War II, and do a little farming. They are literally feudal serfs of a few large landowners. Their economic plight makes them a discontented, rebellious element in Syrian politics.

They dress like the other Arabs with some exceptions; their married women wear a turban from which a stuffed cloth horn protrudes over their foreheads like the horn of a rhinoceros. Their short embroidered jackets worn over gay print dresses with a bright sash at the waist remind one of the costumes of eighteenth-century Turkish women.

Along the northern border is still another sect, the Yezidis. They are Kurds, originally from the mountains west of the Caspian Sea, who have lived in Syria for several centuries. Although they are Sunni Muslims, their religion has become tinged with ideas from Persia, with worship of Satan, who is referred to as "Angel Peacock," and with a bit of ancestor worship from China. They have an organized clergy under an hereditary sheikh, which is unusual in Islam.

These Kurds, of whom Saladin is the most famous, are of larger frame and darker skin than their Arab neighbors. The latter are convinced that the Yezidis are Devil worshippers because they shun the protective color, blue.

In the northeast corner of Syria, called the Jezire, are a number of villages of Turkomen. They are Circassians originating in the mountains east of the Caspian Sea. A sturdy, heavy-built people, they are light-complected with fair hair and blue eyes. Their broad faces, high cheekbones, and slightly folded eyelids indicate Mongol ancestry. They were forcibly moved into Syria by Sultan Abdul Hamid toward the end of the nineteenth century.

Their villages of clustered square houses of dark stone or of mud brick with flattened domes appear rather dreary. But the people are not. They indulge in tobacco and alcohol and love any excuse for a party. The women dress in bright silks with small jackets of contrasting colors. On their heads they wear high wrapped turbans with pompons in front, reminding one of Indian rajahs. The women take an active part in village life and join the men in dancing the traditional *debke,* something the more conservative Arab women would never do.

Turkomen women and men ready to dance the debke.

In the mountains in the southwest corner of Syria is a group of people called the Druze. Their secret religion is thought to be a blend of Muslim and Christian elements. Only a few men who learn the ritual are initiated into the final secret rites. The two hundred thousand or more people are divided into ten great families each ruled by its own amir, or chief. They have played an important part in history: for three hundred years, until the middle of the nineteenth century, Druze princes ruled much of Lebanon and southern Syria. They are still a strong political force there. In 1925 they revolted against French administration. Shelled out of Damascus, they retreated to their old mountain strongholds in southwest Syria and successfully held off the French until a truce was arranged two years later.

South of the Euphrates lies the great northern Arabian desert stretching for hundreds of miles. An arbitrary line drawn on the map cuts diagonally across the desert to form the border with Iraq and Jordan. The desert is not the white sandy waste of Hollywood movies, but a barren expanse of clay, flints, and shale, broken by low mountain ranges and wadis or eroded gullies. Hot in summer, cold in winter, continuously windswept, it is the home of the nomad Bedouin tribes. Their black-tent encampments move with the seasons, following the meager grass.

Among the earliest converts to Islam, the Bedouins are a proud, fierce people who, like their Saudi Arab neighbors to the south, have learned to live off a desert land. The aristocracy breed the famed Arab horses and racing camels as well as the plodding burden-bearing camels. They look down on the sheep-raising tribes. Both are

Bedouin camels at a water hole.

equally contemptuous of the goatherders living on the fringe of the desert, who are considered in the same low class as the despised village dwellers.

For untold centuries the Bedouins have lived by raising stock, bartering with the townsmen, extorting protective taxes from passing caravans, and warring with other tribes. Raids to steal camels, horses, or women were considered good clean fun, and surprisingly few people actually were hurt. Most men and women dress in black clothing. The young bachelors let their hair grow long and then braid it into four "love locks." They are very superstitious, decking themselves and their animals with blue beads to ward off the evil eye.

The governments of Syria, Jordan, and Iraq are now trying to settle the tribes in agricultural communities. Naturally the proud tribesmen are reluctant to give up their carefree drifting with the grazing seasons, racing their camels or horses, or hunting desert hares and gazelles with their falcons. They love to sit around the campfires in the evening drinking bitter black coffee and listening to the storyteller spin long tales of brave old heroes and beautiful sloe-eyed heroines. The old ways were much more fun than being restricted to a dull farmer's life.

There are a bewildering number of Christian sects in Syria, the sum total of Christians somewhere around four hundred fifty thousand, or about ten per cent of the population. Statistics can be only guesses in the Middle East as everyone naturally hates to stand up and be counted by the tax collector. The largest group is the Greek Orthodox, numbering about one hundred forty thousand, with the Armenian Orthodox next, with one hundred thousand. Then there are the Greek Catholics and Syriac Orthodox, each numbering about forty-five thousand. Armenian and Syriac Catholics have about thirty thousand each. The Nestorians and Protestant sects each total about ten thousand and there are a few thousands each of the Latins, Chaldeans, and Maronites. The large body of Maronites is now settled in northern Lebanon.

The Armenians proudly claim that they have been Christians longer than any other racial group. There are about sixty thousand left in Syria from the quarter of a million that fled from Turkey during the nationalist uprising of 1919 to 1921. In the subsequent years most of the Armenians have migrated to other lands, particularly to the United States. In Syria they feel that they are a minority group in an alien land. This migration is Syria's loss, for they are a skillful, hard-working people, clever in mind and hand. Armenians fill most of the professions and provide the skilled mechanics and metal workers.

The Nestorians, or Assyrians as they are called, are refugees from the vicious persecutions in Persia in 1932. They, too, claim to be the first people converted to Christianity after the apostolic age and speak of their religion as the "Church of the East." In their early religious enthusiasm they sent missionaries to establish churches as far east as India and China, and were said to have nearly converted the great Genghis Khan. Marco Polo, writing in the fourteenth century, mentions seeing their churches all along the Great-Caravan route.

There are about twenty-five thousand Jews still living in Syria in spite of the trouble with Israel. Their rights are respected, and they mingle as equals with Christians and Muslims in the business and professional world. They have their synagogues for worship. Free to engage in business as merchants and skilled craftsmen, they are only restricted from military areas.

In the mountains near Damascus there are three villages, Malloula, Isbadeen, and Bajhaa, where the people still use the old Aramaic language spoken by Jesus and his contemporaries. From ancient Persian times, Aramaic was the commercial language throughout the Middle East. It was not until the second century after Christ that Greek became the more common trade language. The survival of Aramaic is testimony to the clannish character of the villages as well as to the deep roots of Syrian culture. Malloula, clinging to a narrow mountain pass, has one of the oldest convents of Christian history. Saint Tekla is considered the guardian of the village and is shown appropriate reverence.

All these religious groups provide subtle differences in costume and customs. As varied as the land itself, the sects offer a rich field for the study of religious history. They also provide an example of amiable tolerance of each other's beliefs. These sects have lived and worked together for centuries with surprisingly little friction. When discord has flared up it was usually instigated by foreign intrigues. On the whole, the people of Syria can be proud of their peaceful history of living and working together.

CHAPTER FOUR

Holy Days and Holidays

THE CHIEF celebrations in Syria and in any other Muslim land concern the last two pillars of Islam.

The ninth month of the Muslim year is called Ramadan, or the month of fasting. Because the Muslims use the lunar calendar, the Fast of Ramadan moves progressively eleven days earlier each year. When the fast occurs in the summer months it becomes an ordeal much more severe than the Christian Lent, or the Jewish Passover, which it resembles.

A religious committee in each country decides when it can first see the new moon, and the word is telegraphed to all the cities. Cannon boom and drums are beaten in the villages.

Then each day at dawn when a white thread can first be distinguished from a black one, the fast begins. The pious Muslim does not eat, drink, or smoke until the guns sound at sunset. Many Muslims wait with a bowl of the "Soup of Ramadan" in their hands, listening for that first boom.

With the end of the long day the family feasts and drinks its fill and then may walk the streets in the brief twilight. Bands of young men stroll about singing songs, each group trying to drown out the other.

Wealthy families will feast all night and sleep through the day. But the workmen will try to get some sleep during the all too short night. By one-thirty during the summer months, the quiet of the neighborhood will be shattered by a man beating a bass drum, clashing cymbals, and singing at the top of his lungs. He is calling the families to rise and eat before the early dawn—a custom surviving from the days before alarm clocks.

About three o'clock the guns boom again and the long day begins. Thirty minutes later, carpenters are hammering, trucks are dumping stones, and peddlers of vegetables, oil, or bread are shouting their wares. All are anxious to get their work done before the intense heat of the day.

Ramadan is nearly as much of a trial of the Christian as of the Muslim. No one gets enough sleep. Exhaustion mounts, tempers fray, and quarrels become more frequent as the days advance. Riots break out over the most trivial causes and the police and ambulances are kept busy.

Muhammed exempted a few persons from the rigor of the fast: young children, pregnant women, the old, the ill, and travelers. Today many of the upper classes take advantage of the rules and pretend to be ill. But the working classes faithfully obey the law. Many collapse and die from heat prostration in the summer.

The end of the month is celebrated with feasting. Called Id el-Fitr, the celebration usually lasts three days. It is a combination of the Christian Christmas and Easter. Everyone appears in new clothes, presents are exchanged, friends make calls and are stuffed with sweetmeats.

The men go to special services at the mosque and the women go to the cemeteries, more to catch up on the gossip than to honor the dead. Schools and business houses close so that everyone can join in the rejoicing. Through it all, drums are beating, radios are blaring, and in the villages the men dance the native debke until exhausted.

The last of the five pillars of Islam is el-Hajji: the pilgrimage to Mecca or Jerusalem, or to both if possible. Every good Muslim is expected to make the pilgrimage at least once during his lifetime. This was not too difficult a feat in Muhammed's day when the faithful lived fairly close to Mecca.

When the Muslim conquest spread Islam from Spain to the Philippines, pilgrimages became a vast and complicated business. The hundreds of thousands of pilgrims today have to be transported to Mecca on time, housed, fed, clothed in their ceremonial robes, and each provided with a sacrificial sheep.

The pilgrimage is held in the twelfth calendar month called Dhu-al-Hijjah. The journeys of the pilgrims must be carefully planned so that they all arrive at the hostels outside Mecca before the sixth day of the month. Weeks before the big event the ports of the Muslim world will be crowded with pilgrims camping on the beaches or on any open space, waiting for the specially charted "pilgrim ships" to arrive.

For hundreds of years, Damascus was the gathering point for pilgrims from Turkey, southern Russia, and Iraq. Camel caravans took at least forty days for the journey from there to Mecca. The short-lived "Pilgrim Railroad" cut the time to five days.

Most of the pilgrims are elderly. Not only has it taken the better part of a lifetime to save enough money to go and return—they will not be admitted to Mecca without showing their return ticket—but there is also a pious hope that the pilgrim may die there and be transported at once to paradise.

Pilgrims are met and housed just outside the Holy City. There they bathe and put on ceremonial clothing consisting of two cotton towels. Women are given a more adequate costume of black and a veil. On the sixth day of the month they enter Mecca, sacred long before Muhammed. Four exhausting days of ritual center around a sacred black stone. Tradition says it was given to Abraham by the Angel Gabriel. Originally white, it has turned black from the sins of man. It is at one corner of a small stone building called the Ka'baa, which originally held the idols destroyed by Muhammed.

The religious ritual includes kissing this stone several times. Processions and prayers include the trial of running from hill to hill in the hot sun. Some of the more aged worshippers achieve their wish for paradise.

The final day, the tenth of Dhu-al-Hijjah, is celebrated throughout the Muslim world. A sheep is sacrificed for a feast; one-third is eaten by the family, one-third is given to relatives, and the last third goes to the poor. A goat, camel, or cow may, if necessary, be substituted, but the sheep is as traditional as the turkey for Thanksgiving or the goose at Christmas.

The trek to Mecca of thousands of pilgrims year after year explains much of the intellectual vigor of the Muslim world while Europe was enduring the so-called Dark Ages. The Muslims were much traveled and were well-informed peoples. At Mecca one met people from many lands and exchanged news and information on a great variety of subjects.

During the days following the ritual in Mecca, the pilgrims begin to return to their homes. Families are notified of their arrival time. Together with friends, they hire taxis and decorate them with palm branches and the families' best rugs. They then go to the edge of the city to await the pilgrim's arrival.

He is now greeted as *al Hajji* and may wear the distinctive green scarf around his head. The family and friends noisily embrace and kiss the returned traveler and escort him to his home.

The doorway has been decorated with palm-leaf arches and, if possible, the house has been outlined with lights. In the Kurdish villages and in Egypt, the doorways will be decorated in colored designs suggesting the journey: gay drawings of camels, boats, donkeys, and airplanes. A sheep is killed before the threshold, and then the whole party goes inside to a feast that has been in preparation for days.

In addition to Ramadan and Id el-Fitr, each of the new Arab nations has acquired holidays of national significance. And parades involving military units, boy and girl scouts, athletic clubs, and children from the various schools march through the main streets.

On the twenty-second of March, annually another holiday honors the formation of the Arab League. April 6 is Martyrs' Day in memory of the twenty-one Arab leaders hanged by the cruel Kamal Pasha, Turkish governor of Syria during the First World War.

Syria has on several occasions declared national days of mourning to remind the people of certain losses and political mistakes. These days are like other traditional holidays except they are celebrated or discarded very much according to the political climate

Girl Scouts parading in Damascus.

of the moment or which party is initiating the holiday. One such day no longer celebrated is November 29, which was set aside at one time to mourn the loss of the province of Hatay and the port of Iskanderun. Another recently discarded is February 22, which was to be an annual day of regret over Syria's union with Egypt in 1958. Now, however, union is again mentioned.

Major holidays among the Christian population are the familiar ones of Easter and Christmas. Celebration used to be complicated by two calendars, Eastern and Western. The Eastern churches, such as the Greek, Armenian, and Nestorian, used the old calendar and celebrated Christmas on what the Western churches call Twelfth Night. Hence the Christmas season lacked that unity of community spirit familiar to Western lands. There were few decorations in the shop windows, no Christmas trees, and no Santa Clauses. Today most churches have adopted the Western calendar and Santa Claus is everywhere. Store windows are decorated with tinsel and Christmas trees are imported from as far away as Europe.

Each of the many Christian groups has its saints' and martyrs' holy days in addition to its celebration of Christmas and Easter. There are also many shrines to be visited by members of the various faiths. One such shrine is unique in that both Christian and Muslim revere Our Lady of Sednaya.

On September 8, the traditional birthday of the Mother of Christ, pilgrims flock to the monastery of Sednaya in the hills twenty-three miles north of Damascus. There in the Greek Orthodox church, reputed to be built on order of the Emperor Justinian in A.D. 546, is an icon or picture of the Virgin Mary holding Christ in her lap. She is surrounded by the faces of the twelve apostles. The icon is said to be the only surviving one of four painted by Saint Luke.

Each year thousands of pilgrims of all faiths visit the church where the holy icon is credited with scores of miraculous cures. The Christian pilgrims light candles while the Muslims leave tin hands of Fatima at the shrine. Even during the bitter struggles of the Crusades, the Muslims permitted Christians to visit the shrine. Two prominent Muslim families still supply the olive oil for the lamps of the sanctuary.

All national groups celebrate their special holidays. The Armenians honor their national hero on Vartan's Day. The British are hosts on the Queen's Birthday and the Americans on the Fourth of July. The British, French, and Americans join in remembering Armistice Day on November 11. A simple but impressive service is held at the military cemeteries kept so immaculately by the British Graves Registration Corps.

Syria, like the rest of the free world, has a number of unexpected holidays. Various guilds strike for higher wages, against the introduction of some labor-saving machinery, or a new policy of the government. Unfortunately the strikes often lead to general riots as was the common practice during the Industrial Revolution of the nineteenth century. Regrettably it is the young students who are incited to leave their classes to demonstrate for the guilds and political parties. All too often the students are the ones to be injured or killed when parades turn into riots.

CHAPTER FIVE

Babylon to Byzantium

SYRIA, forming the western end of the Fertile Crescent, shared in all the early history of the Mesopotamian civilizations. The migrations of peoples, the organization of city-states, and the rise and fall of empires affected Syria as surely as they did the lower Euphrates plains.

This early history of the Middle East is fascinating, but the story belongs to history books and the Old Testament accounts in the Bible. There is very little visual evidence left in Syria to recall these thousands of years of history; no great ruins of temples, palaces, or fortresses remain. But trade goods, pottery, glassware, and other artifacts lie at the bottom of tells, waiting to be uncovered to reveal the story of widespread trade among the peoples of this ancient land.

Syria was fairly peaceful until a people in eastern Asia Minor, the Hittites, were strong enough to push through the Taurus Mountains and found an empire lasting from about 1460 to 1220 B.C. They had iron weapons, harder than bronze, and free-wheeling chariots. The open plains of Syria offered easy conquest. The land was organized into city-states, but the people were permitted a large amount of local authority and freedom to worship their local gods.

Consequently many of these little states survived long after the Hittite Empire collapsed. The Hittites' awesome sculptures, in black basalt, of lions, bulls, gods, and goddesses are found all over north Syria. The massive black figures with staring white marble eyeballs struck the ancient worshippers with terror. Even today the visitor to the National Museum in Aleppo feels a shiver run down his spine as he gazes at these gods of the past.

Conquering peoples flowed and ebbed across the land, molding the inhabitants into composite forms with distinctive noses and an inherited skill in bargaining peculiar to the Middle Easterners of today. Their Phoenician ancestors were particularly skillful traders, who sailed from their coastal cities to roam the Mediterranean Sea.

One such Phoenician city was rediscovered in 1929 and has been carefully excavated by French archaeologists. Ras Shamra, or Ugarit, as it was known in ancient times, proved to have been a great com-

A Hittite lion with fearsome eyes.

mercial city. The houses of her wealthy merchants each had its own well, bath, courtyard, and burial vault. The palace, a huge complex of sixty rooms around two large courtyards, is the largest yet discovered in the Middle East.

Even more important was the discovery of a wealth of clay tablets inscribed in a cuneiform script using a thirty-letter alphabet. This early alphabet, passed on to the Arameans about 800 B.C., was in turn passed along, with modifications, to the Arabs, Indians, and Armenians. It provided workable written languages.

The gift of a written language was the one lasting blessing in centuries of invasion, conquest, and slaughter as one people after another occupied Syria. It was not until Alexander the Great and his Greek armies swept triumphantly through the Middle East to the land of India that a visible impression was made on Syria.

In the short span of eleven years, Alexander founded new cities, built roads and canals, and dedicated temples to both Greek and Eastern gods. After his death in 323 B.C. the vast territory was divided among his generals. Seleucus I became king of Syria and Mesopotamia. The Seleucid rulers, although varying in administrative ability, were consistent builders of cities and temples in a form that blended the rather cold classic lines of Greece with the warmer, more voluptuous designs of the East. The resulting blend, a distinctive style found throughout Syria, is called Hellenistic. Syrian stonemasons became famed for their skill and were in great demand as artisans throughout the Mediterranean world for centuries to come.

One of the Seleucids, Antiochus III, king of Syria from 223 to 187 B.C., using Indian elephants as a modern general would use tanks, recovered all of the Middle East. Then he rashly challenged Roman might, only to be driven out of Asia Minor. Twenty years later Antiochus IV proscribed Judaism as a religion and provoked the revolt of the Jews under Judas Maccabeus. The Jewish subjects had welcomed such Hellenistic innovations as Greek clothing and gymnasiums, but refused to substitute Baal for Jehovah or to relinquish the temple treasures for Antiochus's own use. The revolt was successful and an independent Jewish state existed for eighty years. Furthermore it sparked other revolts that broke up the Seleucid Empire and paved the way for the Armenians to overrun Syria in 83 B.C.

Fourteen years later, the Romans drove the Armenians out of Syria and reinstated the Seleucid princes. But by 64 B.C., the Roman general Pompey, disgusted with the treachery and intrigues of the Seleucids, seized all of Syria and made it a Roman province.

Soon the pride of the Roman Empire, the province of Syria, produced the finest wines, olive oil, wheat, and fruits to supply Roman tables. Syrian ships monopolized the sea routes and carried Hellenistic ideas in architecture, sculpture, and religions, as well as trade goods, to the far corners of the Empire. As the seat of many old religions and the birthplace of a new one, Christianity, the province of Syria became a most important part of the Roman Empire.

A stretch of old Roman road.

Syria even provided a series of emperors beginning with Septimius Severus, who was elected emperor in A.D. 193 through the efforts of his Syrian wife, Julia Domna of Homs. Their elder son, called Caracalla from the coats he introduced to Roman society, murdered his brother and became emperor. He was so cruel, vicious, and incompetent that Julia Domna actually ruled the Empire.

Caracalla was murdered by his soldiers and a nephew Elagabalus was declared emperor through the influence of his grandmother, sister of Julia Domna. He was a fourteen-year-old delinquent who introduced eastern luxuries and vices to horrified Roman society. His extravagances and vices provoked the Praetorian Guard to murder him in A.D. 222 and elect a cousin, Alexander Severus, as emperor. He was the one bright light in this Syrian dynasty: charming, frugal, studious, but weak. Again it was the Syrian women who continued to rule, even taking part in the senate debates. But an attempt to curb the power of the Praetorian Guard led to a revolt and the murder of the entire family.

After nine years of rival claimants and general chaos, the Eastern army proclaimed Philip, the Arab, emperor in 244. Born in the southern Syrian city of Bosra, he rose from the ranks to command the army and then to become emperor. By one of those quirks of history, it was this Syrian upstart who presided over the festivities celebrating the thousandth anniversary of the founding of Rome.

Again, according to what had become a custom, the army revolted and Philip was killed in A.D. 249. His death ended this curious line of alien emperors. They were, with the exception of Alexander Severus, a vicious, cruel, and vindictive lot. But their women were magnificent. Beautiful, charming, intelligent, these Syrian mothers had the brains and audacity to rule an empire with daring and wisdom.

Syria was little affected by the decline of the Empire in the succeeding years. Nor did the division of the Empire in the fourth century and the founding of the Eastern capital at Constantinople make much difference to her people. While nominally under Byzantine rule, the Syrian princes paid little heed to Constantinople. Syria was being torn by the growth of divergent Christian sects drifting apart on questions of dogma, language, and ritual. Church councils, called to reconcile religious differences, only seemed to emphasize and intensify the quarrels. Many Christians retreated to caves, renouncing the world and its disorder. Others banded together in monasteries under a variety of rules of their own making. When Muslim invaders arrived in Syria in the seventh century, many of the people were glad to embrace a new religion and a way of life as yet devoid of petty quarrels over ritual and hair-splitting questions of theology.

CHAPTER SIX

The Flame of Islam

MUHAMMED, founder of Islam, was born in Mecca, Arabia, about
A.D. 570. The story of his career and the establishment of a new way
of life for his desert companions is told in every textbook on world
history. His Hegira, or retreat from Mecca to the more hospitable
city of Medina in 622 has set that date as the year one of the Muslim
calendar.

The Mediterranean world, pagan and Christian, was ripe for a
messiah providing a clearly defined way of life on earth leading to
salvation in the world beyond. Conquest and conversion by the sword
only applied to pagans. Christians and Jews, "People of the Book,"
who shared the Old Testament and its saints with the Koran, were
permitted to follow their own beliefs on payment of a special tax.
With a tolerance unusual in that age or this, the Christians were
merely requested not to carry arms or ring their church bells loudly.

On Muhammed's death, Abu-Bekr was elected caliph, or head of
the faith, according to the tribal custom of electing the most capable
man. Unfortunately he was an old man and died two years later.
Omar was chosen next and showed energetic leadership. His armies

conquered Egypt, Persia, and Palestine.

By the year 635 the Muslim armies had defeated the Byzantines and captured Damascus and the adjacent cities of Homs and Hama, as well as the coastal cities. The year 640 saw all of Syria as far north as the Taurus Mountains under Muslim control. A young Arab general, Mu'awiyah, was appointed governor with his capital at Damascus. His enlightened and tolerant policy won the loyalty of all his subjects most of whom were still Christians. His wife was a Christian as were many of his court officials.

In 661, Mu'awiyah was elected caliph of the Muslim world. He founded the famous Umayyad dynasty that brought glory to Damascus and Syria. On his deathbed, Mu'awiyah designated his son, Yazid, to be his successor. This declaration broke the tribal custom of election and established the hereditary principle of Muslim dynasties to be followed thereafter.

Throughout Umayyad rule the caliphs were noted for their tolerance in religious matters. Many talented Christians held high offices and some were appointed governors; for years Greek was the official language. Several Umayyads had Christian wives who were permitted to keep their faith.

The soft and pleasant living lured these sons of the desert from the strict Muslim virtues. Dicing, horseracing, and hunting became popular. For the latter, hunting lodges, really little palaces, were built in the desert. Gay parties hunted with falcons and selukis. Later cheetahs were introduced from India, as was the game of polo. Wine and poetry flowed at the banquets.

During the reign of the Umayyad caliphs from 661 to 750, Damascus was the pulsing heart of the Muslim world. Her armies carried the Prophet's faith and flag from the Atlantic coast to the Indus River of India, from the Aral Sea in the north to the cataracts of the Nile in the south. These conquests covered an area greater than that of the Roman Empire at its largest extent.

The tide of Islam was finally stopped in its westward flood by

Charles Martel at Tours in 732. His army of Christian knights fought the Muslim invaders of Gaul and pushed them back across the Pyrenees into Spain. This event had repercussions as far away as Damascus.

The Umayyads, who were never popular outside of Syria, were held responsible for the defeat. A conspiracy was formed in Iraq to support the Shi'ite Abbasids and overthrow the Umayyads.

Marwan, the last of the thirteen caliphs of Damascus, led an army into northern Iraq to quell the rebellion. A nine-day battle ended in Marwan's defeat. He fled to Egypt where he was killed and his head sent to the victorious Abu-al-Abbas, leader of the rebellion. The family of the Umayyads and their followers were hunted down and killed, Umayyad tombs destroyed, and all Umayyad inscriptions chiseled from the public buildings.

A new Muslim caliphate of the Abbasids was established at Kufah on the lower Euphrates, but later moved to Baghdad. Syrian officials at Damascus were replaced by Persians and the glory of the Umayyad court was gone from Damascus forever.

The three hundred and fifty years that elapsed from the end of the Umayyad caliphate to the first of the Crusades saw Syria torn by dissension. The old easy relationship between Christian and Muslim, based on mutual respect, was replaced by indignities and persecutions. Christians and Jews were required to wear a distinctive yellow garb, to put wooden images of devils on their houses, and to level their graves to the ground. They could ride only on asses or donkeys and had to use a peculiar wooden saddle. In addition to these embarrassments they had to pay a heavy poll tax. While the strict enforcement of these regulations varied with the temper of the governor, they made the large Christian population restless and unhappy, ready to join with the Syrian Muslims in the many attempts at rebellion against the hated Abbasids of Baghdad.

By the tenth century there were separate caliphates in Spain, Egypt, and Arabia. In Syria the jealousy and ambition of the feudal princes led to constant raiding against one another. At the end of the tenth century the Byzantine prince, Nicephorus Phocas, felt strong enough to lead a large army into Syria. Aleppo, Apamea, Homs, Hama, and Damascus were recaptured. Antioch alone was spared as an ancient Christian city. Tripoli withstood all attacks. The Byzantines, loaded with loot, drew back of the protective range of the Taurus Mountains.

The next invaders of Syria came from the east. The Seljuks, a Turkish tribe, migrated westward from Turkestan. On the way they came in contact with and accepted the Sunni rather than the Shi'ite version of Islam. The Seljuk hordes overran Mesopotamia and Syria with little opposition. By 1071 they defeated the Byzantine army and all Asia Minor was their prize.

The Seljuk prince Ridwan occupied Aleppo in 1095 and his brother Duqaq became lord of Damascus. It was these Seljuk lords and their companions who were soon to be attacked by the Crusaders. They and the lesser Arab princes, quarreling among themselves, failed to present a united front to the Western invaders. This lack of unity gave the Crusaders their early, easy conquest of the Holy Land.

CHAPTER SEVEN

Cross and Crescent

THE ROMANTIC STORY of the Crusades, Western Christian attempts to reoccupy the Holy Land, is well known. Christian successes were helped by the civil war among the Seljuk princes. The Armenian Christian population of southern Asia Minor also aided in establishing a Burgundian principality at Edessa and a Norman state at Antioch. The county of Tripoli was held by knights from Provence.

The Kingdom of Jerusalem was established after the capture of the city on July 15, 1099. Here the Burgundians were also the strongest party. These sectional rivalries and feudal loyalties were to prevent any united front against a rising Muslim strength.

For the next two hundred years the Franks, as the Arabs and Turks called them, kept a precarious hold on the coastal lands of Syria and Palestine. The Franks, however, failed to push through the mountains and capture either Damascus or Aleppo, key cities to the control of the great caravan route. Consequently the Crusaders were held to the narrow coastal plain and became more and more dependent on Western cargo ships for supplies and ultimately for desperate survival. After the first invasion overland, the effective reinforcements came by the water route. Men, horses, and supplies were freighted by the fleets of Venice and Genoa. These cities grew wealthy on the traffic and became bitter rivals for monopoly of the trade routes.

Meanwhile the Crusaders lost ground under the attacks of the Saracens, reinforced by the fresh enthusiasm of the Seljuk Turks. One of their number was the great Salah-al-Din, known to the Franks as Saladin. He drove the Crusaders out of Jerusalem and seized their castles one by one, until only the port cities remained in Christian hands.

The succeeding years saw these ports and their castles besieged and captured, as help failed to arrive from Europe. With the fall of Acre in May of 1291, and the slaughter of the garrison, the few remaining Frankish strongholds at Tyre, Sidon, and Beirut were abandoned. Only the old Phoenician island stronghold of Arwad, held by the Templars, survived for another eleven years. Then they, too, retreated to join their fellow Franks on the island of Cyprus.

The early Crusader princes who took feudal lands for themselves got along surprisingly well with their Arab neighbors. A spirit of mutual respect and tolerance only occasionally flared into quarrels. On the other hand the military orders were bitter foes of the Arabs. The Knights Hospitalers had been organized long before the Crusades to provide hostels, hospitals, and protection to pilgrims going to Jerusalem. The Knights Templars were also a military order formed in 1118 to defend the Temple in Jerusalem. Each order had its own grand master responsible only to the pope in Rome.

Both orders, dedicated to war on the "infidels," were intolerant of any compromise. As the years wore on, the two orders became rich, powerful, and arrogant. They assumed defense of the castles as the Crusader wave began to recede. Fanatical in their hatred of the Muslims, they felt that time was wasted when they were not fighting either their enemies or, sad to say, each other.

Much to their surprise the Crusaders found an older, more cultured society among the Saracens than the one they had known at home. Some of the knowledge and culture rubbed off on the families that settled in the Holy Land. When they were forced to leave, they took the newly acquired customs with them.

They took back to Europe strange new fabrics such as muslin, taffeta, silk, and damask. They had learned, the hard way, to appreciate the superiority of Damascus steel for weapons. Their eyes had been dazzled by the tapestries, gold and silver jewelry, pottery, glass, and tooled-leather goods. Their womenfolk, charmed with the soft, smooth dress fabrics, were equally delighted with the East's exotic perfumes.

Many of the devices of heraldry were borrowed from the Saracens who used such designs as beasts and flowers to identify their weapons and property. Some of the names still used in heraldic language are of Arabic origin, as are so many names of the stars.

Through contacts with the Muslims here and in Spain, Europeans were introduced to a variety of delicious foods. Lemons, dates, pomegranates, strawberries, sugar cane, oranges, apricots, bananas, and peaches augmented the usually dull Frankish menu. Through Muslim exporters, Europeans learned of rice and buckwheat from China, delicious melons from Persia, and spices from India. The windmill was introduced to Europe to become a common feature of the landscape. Paper came by way of Spain to Europe in the twelfth century in plenty of time for Gutenberg and his printing press.

In the sciences, the Arabs' contributions in mathematics, astronomy, and navigation are too numerous to detail. European sailors blessed the astrolabe, the compass, and the lanteen sail that made navigation easier and safer.

It was by military architecture, however, that the Crusaders were most impressed. The details one thinks of as "castle-like" were largely borrowed from the Saracens, who had inherited them with their conquest of Syria. The saw-toothed battlements, pointed archways, round towers supporting and strengthening the walls, the portcullis and block-S or right-angled entrance, are but a few of the ideas taken back to strengthen and improve European castles.

All too many of the Arab castles have served as handy quarries for building stone and are now gone. But a handsome example of Arab military architecture, with all its distinctive features, remains in Aleppo. The castle, or Citadel, is built on a huge tell that rises in the center of the city. Ghazi, son of Saladin, dug a moat 100 feet wide and 60 feet deep and paved it and the steep sides of the tell with cut stone as smooth as glass to make a climbing attack impossible.

The walls around the top enclose an oval area 1100 by 800 feet, which could house a garrison of ten thousand. Towers at regular intervals strengthened the walls and provided the opportunity to shoot along the walls. The huge moat below has a square-guard tower protecting the causeway and a second entrance tower big enough to contain a throne room above.

The actual entrance, protected by an iron portcullis, is shaped like a block S. At every bend are slits for bowmen to shoot the

Aleppo's Citadel looms above the courtyard in the Great Mosque.

The entrance gateways to Aleppo's Citadel.

helpless attacker. Above each bend, the ceiling provides holes through which to pour boiling oil, lead, quicklime, and other unpleasant things on the heads below.

On the face of the gate tower, small boxlike projections are provided with holes between the brackets. Defenders above the gate could shoot arrows or pour oil on any enemy threatening the gate.

The entrance slopes up to a street on top of the tell. It was once lined with shops that extended the length of the enclosure. Two mosques, a royal palace with baths, and a later Egyptian barracks seem lost in the huge walled area. The many structures now gone must have made it a bustling city in itself.

The Crusaders were quick to appreciate the military advantages in this type of architecture and to add the new ideas to their own castles. In various stages of ruin Crusader castles dot the rocky foothills and shores of the eastern Mediterranean coast. Built within signaling distance of each other, many stand boldly against the sky like land-bound battleships. Carefully chosen spurs of rock provided the steep slopes so necessary to defense. Consequently most of the land castles are like an A in plan. The upper half of the A would point aggressively at the plains and sea below. The bar of the A would be heavily walled against attack from the gentler slope of the mountains behind.

The Krak des Chevaliers, or Castle of the Knights, is the best preserved example of Crusader military architecture. It guards the mountain pass from the ports of Antioch and Tartous to Homs and the caravan routes of the interior. Its position, remote from any town, has saved it from the plundering that has ruined many others.

The Knights Hospitalers built the huge fortress as it stands today. It could be approached only from the usual rocky base of the A, which was protected by a moat and double walls. The sharp point of the A is still crowned by a high wall protected and strengthened by large round towers.

The Krak des Chevaliers from the air.

The main entrance on the east flank is perched above a steep hill that offered no opportunity for direct assault. Inside, the vaulted passage, narrow and climbing, doubles back on itself. A portcullis and numerous slits gave the defenders command of every foot of the way. Inside the first walls, a moat full of water further protects another mountain of stone sloping up to tremendous battlements.

Within this huge castle there was room for two thousand knights with their squires and horses. One vaulted chamber, four hundred feet long, housed the men-at-arms. A courtyard provided ample space for exercise and jousting. Above it are the graceful arched chambers of the grand master, who could look down on the yard bustling with knights and archers. The tremendous size of the castle and the resulting sense of power are overwhelming. Today the huge emptiness awes the visitor and increases the feeling of being alone, desolate, on a ship plowing off into uncharted seas.

The Krak was never taken by assault. In 1163 the Emir Nur-ed-Din and his huge army were routed by a sudden sortie of the Knights during the siesta hour. A generation later the great Saladin paused before the forbidding fortress and turned away. It was not until 1271 that the Sultan Baybars, with an Egyptian army and help from the grand master of the Assassins, attacked the castle. By hard fighting, the lower town and two outer walls were taken, but the mass of the inner fort remained secure. Finally treachery achieved what force could not. A forged letter, presumed to be from the grand commander of Knights Hospitalers at Tripoli, ordered the knights of the Krak to surrender. They did as ordered and were given safe conduct to the coast by the sultan. The fortress that held off the enemy for 161 years at last fell into the hands of the Muslims.

Other Crusader castles in Syria in a fair state of preservation are Saone, Margat or Merkab, and Tortosa. The first two are difficult to reach, a fact which explains their preservation. Lesser castles, towers, and chapels dot the coastal plains to remind one of the stirring but futile years spent here by the Crusaders.

CHAPTER EIGHT

Mamluke, Mongol, and Ottoman

THE GREAT SALADIN wanted to unite Egypt and Syria, make the Sunni sect of Islam supreme, and carry out a jihad, or holy war against the Franks. He succeeded in all three goals but the effort was exhausting. He fell an easy victim to fever at the age of fifty-five and was buried in Damascus in 1193.

By his will, Saladin's three sons were to inherit the lands of Syria, Palestine, and Egypt. But family jealousies allowed these territories to break up into a number of small principalities. Military fervor waned, to be replaced by a zeal for building palaces, mosques, and *madrassas,* or schools.

Two new forces were waiting in the wings to occupy the Syrian stage. They were the Mamlukes and the Mongols. The Mamlukes were Circassian and Turkish slaves who had been trained as a select body of warriors by Saladin's successors. By the time St. Louis of France invaded Egypt in 1248, the Mamlukes were a superb fighting force that easily annihilated the French army and captured King Louis.

The Mamlukes, dissatisfied with their share of the booty, revolted, deposed the caliph of Egypt, and for nearly three hundred years ruled Egypt and Syria. This line of Mamluke caliphs is unique in history for each one was elected for his military prowess. A slave today might be the caliph tomorrow. For the most part they were an uncultured and bloodthirsty lot who ruled by the sword. Yet they

The Mausoleum of Saladin.

did succeed in pushing the last of the Crusaders out of Syria and twice turned back the Mongol hordes.

The Mongols, hard-riding, hard-fighting, nomad tribes of central Asia, had been welded into a mobile army under the great Genghis Khan. By the middle of the thirteenth century the Mongol armies had overrun Asia Minor. Hulagu, grandson of Genghis Khan, captured and sacked Baghdad in 1258 and executed the last Abbasid caliph, Musta'sim. Next, he invaded Syria, captured the city of Aleppo, and besieged the Citadel. By treachery some fifty thousand persons were put to the sword. In quick succession Damascus, Homs, Hama, and Antioch were taken.

In 1260 a Mamluke army under the great general Baybars crushed the Mongol army and drove it out of Syria. Baybars expected the sultan to give him Aleppo as a reward. When he was disappointed, he stabbed the sultan in the neck and took the title himself. By 1271 he had captured the major Crusader strongholds, one by one. Antioch alone supplied one hundred thousand captives to be sold as slaves. The Krak, Merkab, and many lesser Frankish castles surrendered.

An administrator as well as a warrior, Baybars restored the damaged castles, built mosques, canals, and improved the harbors. Egypt and Syria were ably governed by the aid of a fast postal-relay service. But this peace and resulting accomplishments proved to be only a lull before the storm.

Again and again the Mongols laid waste the land of Syria. In the year 1400, Tamerlane took Aleppo, slaughtering twenty thousand of its inhabitants. For the first time the great Citadel was taken by storm after Tamerlane had deliberately sacrificed enough of his army so that the corpses could be used to fill the moat and provide an easy causeway to the walls.

Damascus held out for a month; then, in betrayal of the surrender terms, the Mongols plundered and burned the city. Over thirty thousand men, women, and children were herded into the Great Mosque, where they perished when the building was set on fire. Only the skilled craftsmen in metal, glass, and weaving were spared and taken to Samarkand to establish new industries there.

Later the Turks challenged the Mamlukes and overwhelmed them with powder and shot. Syria was quickly occupied and much Mamluke treasure seized. A final campaign against Egypt in 1517 again proved the superiority of Turkish arms. Egypt along with the Arabian peninsula became part of the Ottoman Empire.

It was unfortunate that the people of Syria, still battered from the Mongol invasions, should now come under Turkish rule. For the next three hundred years, Syrians were to experience bad government, oppression, and exorbitant taxation. Nor was that all, for soon Vasco da Gama was to open a new sea route to India and the Far East. Columbus discovered a new world that drew European trade to the new West.

The result of these events was the ruin of Syria's economy. For centuries Aleppo had been the terminus of the Great Caravan route

Silk yarn merchants in the souk.

Weaving on a hand loom.

from India and China. Smaller caravans took the merchandise from Aleppo south to Egypt, north to Byzantium, and west to the coast. From there ships sailed to the great ports of Europe. Aleppo's eighteen miles of vaulted *souks,* or streets of little shops built in the thirteenth century, testify to the volume of caravan trade that existed before the new sea routes were discovered.

Damascus was more fortunate than Aleppo. The city continued to profit from the business of organizing the annual pilgrimage to Mecca. But her steel making had been crippled by the Mongols. One family alone still knew the secret of putting enamels on copper and continued to make beautiful bowls, trays, and incense burners. The farmers of the oasis went on producing food, and weavers worked the looms in Homs and Hama. But all the cities and villages were feeling the effects of Ottoman misrule and the competition of the new sea routes.

Under the Ottoman system, the sultan became the head of both religion and government. He appointed pashas who governed the provinces. Under the corrupt Turkish system the pashas bought their offices. They then extorted their personal fortunes out of the unfortunate subjects. Centuries of corruption, tyranny, and excessive taxation left most Syrian families stripped of their wealth, cowed and helpless under governors from whom there was no appeal or redress.

The Turkish officials had little cultural effect on the people of Syria. They did not attempt to colonize Syria. Arabic remained the language of the land although Turkish was the language of officials and courts. Few people bothered to learn more than the basic words of Turkish needed for greetings.

The nineteenth century saw the Ottoman Empire begin to crumble. When Napoleon pulled his troops out of Egypt in 1801, the sultan's general Mehemed Ali declared himself ruler of Egypt. His son Ibrahim Pasha drove the Turkish forces out of Syria in 1833. Only British intervention blocked the formation of a large Arab state. British naval bombardments forced Ibrahim Pasha to retire to Egypt in 1841, leaving Syria again to Turkish rule.

After Ibrahim Pasha had been forced to give up Syria, the sultan of Turkey restored all the petty restrictions so hated by the Christian minorities. In 1860 the Druze, encouraged by the Turks, fell on the Maronite Christians. Horrible massacres occurred in Damascus and in many villages. Napoleon III sent a French army and posed as the champion of the Christians. Commercial jealousy prompted Britain to turn on her recent ally and aid the Druze. The French troops were withdrawn after a year. By agreement, Lebanon was made a separate administrative district under a Christian governor appointed by the sultan and ratified by Great Britain and France. There was no such relief for the rest of Syria.

CHAPTER NINE

The Arab Renaissance

ARABIC LEARNING, once so influential, lay smothered under Turkish despotism. What schools survived were content to have the students memorize verses from the Koran. The students chanted the verses in unison. The louder the chanting the more successful the schooling.

However, the early nineteenth century witnessed a reawakening, or renaissance, of intellectual curiosity. An Arabic press, set up in Cairo in 1822, started printing books by contemporary writers as well as reprinting older Arabic classics.

Ibrahim's enlightened and tolerant rule of Egypt and Syria encouraged the American missionaries to set up a printing press at Beirut, in 1834. French missionaries followed suit nineteen years later. Their press was used to further the spread of French faith and culture, whereas the American mission press printed foreign textbooks in Arabic. Furthermore the American missionaries preached and taught in Arabic; encouraged their students to study their own Arabic literature and take pride in their Arabic heritage.

In 1860, the destruction following the Muslim-Druze war forced the missionaries to add orphanages to their schools. They then greatly broadened their Western influence. Hospitals were founded by the European and American missions in the larger cities. In 1866, the Syrian Protestant College was founded, to be known after 1920 as the American University of Beirut. Accepting students from all lands and faiths, the college had much to do with freeing students' minds from the chains of tradition.

Meanwhile the press in Cairo had been pouring out Arabic classics that were eagerly read by the educated youths. As early as 1847, a Society of Arts and Sciences was founded in Beirut. While open to all faiths, it was dedicated to Arabic rather than Turkish culture.

Ibrahim Yaziji, a poet, and Butrus Bustani are considered the fathers of Arab nationalism in Syria. Both came from prominent Arab-Christian families. Bustani and an American missionary, Eli Smith, together translated the Bible into Arabic, a ten-year task.

In 1860, Bustani started a school with Yaziji as headmaster. Their purpose was to teach religious tolerance and Arab unity. Students spread their ideals throughout Syria and did much to calm religious strife after the war. The foreign schools also added their support to the concepts of tolerance and unity. In the classrooms and on the campuses, the students were daily practicing the ideals and absorbing the lessons of democracy and self reliance.

The ideas of tolerance, democracy, Arab unity, and independence were dangerous thoughts to hold in the last quarter of the nineteenth century. Abdul Hamid's secret police were everywhere and young men had to be very careful not to be overheard when discussing such radical ideas. Many youths studying abroad stayed there to promote the idea of Arab unity by publishing magazines to be smuggled into their homelands.

Nor were the Arabs alone in their hatred of Abdul Hamid's oppressive despotic rule. As early as 1891 young Turkish students were secretly organizing with the hope of reforming and modernizing the Turkish government. Popularly known as the "Young Turks," they were finally strong enough to effect an army revolt in 1908. Hamid was forced to restore the constitution of 1876 he had so long ignored. Censorship of the press was removed and all political prisoners were freed. A year later Hamid was deposed and a puppet sultan installed as religious head of Islam but without any political power.

The Arabs of Syria were jubilant. They had hoped for the creation of an Arab-Turkish state patterned on the dual monarchy of Austria-Hungary with the latter semi-independent. But the Arabs and the minority groups soon learned they had merely exchanged one despot for a committee of despots. The Young Turks' reforms did not include recognition of minority groups. Even the territorial losses of the Balkan Wars did not shake their brand of Turkish nationalism.

By the time the World War broke in 1914, the Turkish provinces of North Africa had been lost to French, Spanish, and Italian colonization. When Turkey became an ally of Germany and Austria, the Arabs of Syria and Arabia' had no choice but to turn to Britain for help to achieve their dreams of independence.

Their chance came when the puppet caliph, set up in Constantinople to act as religious head of Islam, proclaimed a jihad, or holy war against all Christian enemies. But it was necessary for him to have the approval of Sharif Husain, head of the Hashamite tribes, who was hereditary custodian of the holy shrine at Mecca. Husain refused to endorse a jihad, much to the relief of England and France. Consequently the Muslim peoples of the Middle East, North Africa, India, and the Far East did not rise to support Turkish ambitions. The centuries old, stupid, and suppressive policies of the Ottoman Empire had left deeper and more bitter resentment than had the comparatively short experience with European colonialism.

The Turkish leaders further enraged the Syrian Arabs by appointing Ahmed Jamel Pasha as commander of the Fourth Army in Syria. He was already infamous for his cruel, ruthless massacres of the Armenian peoples who had demonstrated in hope of independence after the 1908 revolution.

Jamel Pasha lived up to his reputation in his administration of Syria. Syrian regiments were transferred to Turkey to be replaced by German and Turkish troops. He further endeared himself to the Syrians by hanging twenty-one prominent Syrian leaders, suspected of heading nationalist societies.

As World War I progressed, the few remaining forests of Syria were cut down to provide fuel to keep the railroads operating from Damascus to Medina. Plagues of locusts ate the crops, food became scarce, and hoarding sent prices soaring. Famine and the added horror of typhus stalked the land and over three hundred thousand persons died in Syria alone.

Jamel Pasha closed the British and French schools and hospitals. Their staffs and some students found refuge on the campus of the Syrian Protestant College in Beirut. It is a tribute to the effective work of the college that it remained open throughout the war. It was also through the efforts of the influential graduates of the college and her sister school, Robert College in Constantinople, that President Woodrow Wilson was persuaded *not* to declare war on Turkey. As a result, supplies could continue to be sent from America to the starving faculty, students, and their families.

When Sharif Husain refused to endorse the jihad, British agents approached him and the affiliated Arab tribes, asking them all to help against the Turks. In return the British government pledged itself to support an independent Arab state in the Arabian peninsula. Sir Henry McMahon, governor-general of Egypt, in an historic note of October 1915, further spelled out Britain's determination to support full Arab independence from the Ottoman Turks.

Sharif Husain, horrified at Jamel Pasha's brutality in Syria, accepted Britain's pledge and one month later started the Arab revolt. British agents helped organize the Arabs into guerrilla bands that harassed the Turkish-German army units in Arabia. Eventually they succeeded in cutting the railroad lines and isolating the garrisons along the route to Mecca, who were forced to surrender.

T. E. Lawrence is the most familiar and famous of the British agents. Ardent supporters and vehement detractors have all written books about the man and his exploits. Particular details aside, he did play an important part in the Arab revolt. After the Arab armies had cut off and stranded the garrisons in Arabia, they swept northward to Damascus to join with the British and French armies in the defeat and annihilation of the Turko-German forces.

General Allenby had organized his attack on Palestine and Syria from his headquarters in Egypt. By the happy discovery that chicken wire laid on the desert would support heavy vehicles, and by using an ever-extended pipeline of fresh water, Allenby was able to cross the Sinai desert. The British army swept up the coast while the Arab forces advanced along the eastern desert route. Combined operations wiped out four Turkish divisions. British and Arab troops joined forces in Damascus.

In the meantime, the secret Sykes-Picot agreement of May 1916 had proposed dividing the Arab lands of the Ottoman Empire into British and French spheres of influence. A year later the Balfour Declaration promised the Zionists a Jewish National Home in Palestine. The Arabs, unaware of this conflict of interests, felt that they had been betrayed when the Bolshevik revolutionaries revealed the Sykes-Picot agreement. Their delegates sent to protest were refused a hearing at Paris. This was a violation of basic Arab law that assures even the lowliest man the right to plead his case before a judge or a king.

The British and Arab armies met in Damascus on October 2, 1918. Within two weeks French forces had taken Beirut and occupied the province of Lebanon. By the end of the month Turkey had agreed to the Armistice of Mudros, to repudiate Germany, demobilize her army, and open Turkish territory and the Straits to Allied occupation. On November 13, 1918, Allied forces took over Constantinople. After 465 years the cross supplanted the crescent in the old capital of Byzantium.

Meanwhile Prince Feisal had been proclaimed emir of Syria. He was a natural choice as the thirty-seventh descendant from the Prophet. It was a cruel shock when the Sykes-Picot agreement was revealed and the Arabs learned that their lands were to be divided between France and Great Britain. Emir Feisal, accompanied by Colonel W. F. Stirling as adviser, went to London to confer with British Prime Minister Lloyd George. His appeals for an independent

Syria were ignored and at the Conference at San Remo, April 25, 1920, it was decided that France would take over Syria and Lebanon. General Henri Gouraud was appointed high commissioner. Emir Faisal was ordered to leave Damascus. After one disastrous battle with the better-armed French troops, he had to retire. French forces entered Damascus and the League of Nations approved the mandate on July 24, 1922.

France had already occupied the province of Lebanon and made Beirut the governmental headquarters. Few Arabs, Muslim or Christian, were happy about the defeat of Arab nationalism. French policy was to divide the country into sanjaks or administrative districts based on religious groupings, the old Roman "divide-and-rule" policy. Sporadic demonstrations and riots flared up throughout the mandate.

Unfortunately General Gouraud, a charming man who had led some American troops in the late war and was popular with the foreign colony in Beirut, was replaced by General Weygand and later by General Sarrail. When General Sarrail arrested and executed a guest of Sultan-el-Atrash, head of the Druze, he violated the Arab laws of hospitality. This violation of tradition resulted in a two-year revolt. In the course of the war most of the older section of Damascus was shelled and destroyed. Many hundreds of lives were lost. The Druze retreated to their mountain stronghold in southwest Syria, and a negotiated treaty a year later finally ended the warfare.

To ease the discontent and rioting, the French administration finally promised to end martial law and call general elections for a constitutional assembly. The Nationalist party won the majority of seats and a constitution was proclaimed May 14, 1930. It provided for a president to hold office for five years, a chamber of deputies elected for four years, and the franchise or right to vote, to all men over twenty years of age.

The next six years were ones of storm and stress with the French high commissioner frequently interfering with or nullifying the work of the chamber. By 1936, the administration realized that they must make concessions to popular unrest, so proposed a Treaty of Perpetual Peace. Syria ratified the treaty but France did not solve the underlying problems causing friction. In 1937 the French administration gave the sanjak of Alexandretta a large amount of local authority. Two years later the French gave the whole rich province to Turkey as a bribe to remain on the side of the Allies if the threats of war turned into another world conflict. Syrians have never forgiven this betrayal and loss of the rich valley of the Hatay and the fine port of Alexandretta, now called Iskanderun.

The Arabs were further angered when, on the fall of France in 1940 in World War II, the administration of Syria sided with the Vichy government. In 1940-41, numbers of Germans infiltrated Syria, raising the suspicion that Egypt would be attacked through Syria. It was not long before the Germans were allowed to use Syrian airports to aid a rebellion in Iraq.

Britain, with the aid of a token force of Free French, moved quickly. In a rapid campaign, troops moved up the Lebanese coast and after some sharp fighting occupied Beirut, Damascus, and Aleppo. The Arabs cared little more for the British than they did for the French, but the occupation brought prosperity. The soldiers spent a lot of money and business boomed. In spite of the prosperity, Arab pride insisted that the foreign armies be withdrawn. The Chambers of Deputies in Lebanon and Syria declared war on Germany on October 14, 1944, and petitioned to attend the forthcoming United Nations' conference. Both countries were invited as sovereign states to the first conference, held in San Francisco in April, 1945.

Britain and France were asked to remove their troops. The French were reluctant to go and fighting broke out in Damascus. Again the French bombed the city, for three days of terror. The British, with the backing of the United States, intervened and forced France to withdraw her troops. England followed suit. April 17, 1946, celebrated as the Day of Liberation, saw the last foreign troops leave Syrian soil. Syria at last was independent.

CHAPTER TEN

Damascus, the Capital

DAMASCUS, capital of Syria, is now a modern city of Mediterranean architecture with over four hundred thousand inhabitants. It lies in an oasis against the Anti-Lebanon Mountains and faces the north Arabian desert. A very old city, it is, according to tradition, the home of Adam, Noah, and Abraham. Here Cain slew Abel; there is a red rock on the hillside to prove it. Successive wars, with their inevitable bombardments, have erased much of the old quarter of the city. Today, the capital is a bustling one of wide boulevards, attractive public buildings, modern apartments, luxury hotels, and smart shops. All of the major countries have embassies and consulates here, which give the city a cosmopolitan look. It is easily accessible by a scenic road from the port of Beirut, and is a popular introduction to the "mysterious East" for the tourists on cruise ships.

The Barada River winds through Damascus and fans out in canals to irrigate the semicircle of orchards and gardens called the *Ghuta*. These gardens of fruits, vegetables, and melons among orchards of olive, almond, and apricot form a green half-circular band some fifteen miles wide. Beyond lies the desert.

84

The great oasis of Damascus was taken by storm by the Muslims in A.D. 635. Half of the city was leveled by an earthquake in Justinian's time, and another even greater one devastated the whole of Syria in 1157. Captured and burned by Hulagu in 1260 and by Tamerlane in 1401, not to recount the lesser riots and disasters, the city has managed to survive all these calamities. It took the modern planes and bombs of the French army to wipe out most of the old quarter of Damascus in the Druze rebellion of 1922.

Damascus became the seat of the new Muslim learning and developing culture. It also became the point of departure for the annual caravans to Mecca. The pilgrims gathered early enough each year so that the caravan could make the long slow journey to Mecca before the holy month of Ramadan. Imagine the excitement: the shouting noisy drivers loading the grumbling, squealing camels, two to four thousand of them to a caravan.

Damascus is a bustling modern city.

On the day of departure, the people would turn out to watch the spectacle. Bands played, friends and relatives shouted farewells and escorted the long column of loaded camels, drivers, and armed guards to the south gateway. Only one who has visited the Middle East can imagine the noise and confusion attending such an event. But what a fine excuse for everyone in Damascus to turn out and make it a holiday!

Damascus is no longer the rally point for the great caravans. First a "pilgrim railroad" and now ships and airplanes have displaced the plodding camel. But Damascus is still a gathering place for the modern pilgrim, the tourist. Much of the city's economy depends on tourist dollars. Luxurious hotels, like the New Semiramis, Cattan, and the New Omayyad, to name only a few, are designed to make every foreign visitor comfortable, well fed, and happy.

The tourist usually goes first to the souk or streets of shops. These shops are covered by corrugated iron roofs that were put up in honor of the visit of the German Kaiser Wilhelm in 1898. The ugly roofs, however, do not discourage the visitors from buying the brocades, leather goods, inlaid wooden boxes, glass, and brassware displayed in the shops.

Close beside the bazaars is the Omayyad, or Great Mosque. Built on the site of the Byzantine Cathedral of St. John, most of which was torn down by Caliph Walid in 705, the large rectangular building with hipped roof and huge dome dominates the skyline of Damascus as does St. Peter's Cathedral in Rome. Measuring 430 by 125 feet, it is next to St. Peter's in size. The caliph was determined to make it the most beautiful mosque in the Muslim world. He spent ten years' revenue on rare marble and mosaic decorations, gold lamps and rich carpets, and added minarets to the courtyard. One wing was built to be exactly 751.5 miles from both Constantinople and Mecca and cost 751,500 piasters.

Unfortunately, a series of earthquakes, fires, and the ravages of war have all left their damage. Only a few sections of the mosaics

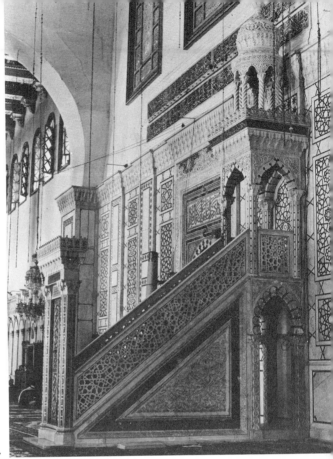

Inside the Omayad Mosque.

remain on the arches in the colonnaded courtyard. Done by imported Greek craftsmen, they show scenes of Damascus, orchards, and villages, a delightful change from stiff Byzantine portraits of saints.

The mosque, however, is still impressive. The huge courtyard contains a bookstall, a fountain for washing, and a treasury. The latter is an octagonal building set up on columns like a water tank; the only entrance is through a trap door. Any aspiring robber would have to bring his own ladder.

Two of the minarets are graceful, spired conversions of the original square bell towers of the Cathedral. The third is a slender round column, the first minaret to be built in the new Muslim style.

Before entering the main building the visitor is given oversized carpet slippers to put over his shoes to protect the precious rugs on the floor. Inside, the open spaciousness of the prayer room awes the visitor. Two rows of graceful columns supporting round arches divide the huge space. Here is also the first *mihrab* or recessed niche to be built to indicate the direction of Mecca. Under the right-hand row of arches is an ornate columned shrine with its own dome. It is supposed to contain the head of John the Baptist, who is also considered a saint by the Muslims.

In spite of the Muslim conquest, Damascus continued to be a great religious center of Christendom for nearly two centuries. The community in the seventh and eighth centuries supplied five popes, two of whom were canonized. John of Damascus (c. 676-748) was the great Christian scholar who fought to keep the images of the saints in the churches. He opposed the Byzantine Emperor Leo the Isaurian, whose icon-smashing has given us the word "iconoclast." Two hymns written by John of Damascus, "The Day of Resurrection" and "Come, Ye Faithful, Raise the Strain" are still to be found in hymn books today.

A short walk along the outer wall of the Great Mosque, and one sees a small courtyard and simple white-domed building that houses the tomb of Saladin. The marble sarcophagus is tastefully decorated with vine patterns and topped with a green cloth tent embroidered with gold. It was a gift of Kaiser Wilhelm of Germany in a bid for Muslim support for his schemes against Great Britain. The original carved wood sarcophagus sits beside it. The simplicity of the little whitewashed building is in character with Saladin's reputation as a warrior-saint who could teach his Christian opponents lessons in

The courtyard of the Azam Palace.

chivalry, humility, and tolerance.

A bit farther on is the eighteenth-century Azam Palace, now the Museum of National Tradition. One enters by a charming colonnaded courtyard. A central pool reflects the graceful pointed arches and alternating bands of black and yellow stone—a style long used in Saracen architecture and copied in the west as, for example, in the jewel-like cathedral of Siena, Italy.

The palace rooms provide a perfect background for the exhibits of furniture and crafts of different districts. Wax figures wearing the old costumes are shown doing the familiar tasks that are appropriate to the various rooms. They make it easy to recapture the reality of gracious living known in the eighteenth century.

Damascus has many famous mosques and madrassas hidden about the city. But the gem of them all is the Sultan Suleyman I Mosque, started in 1554 on the river bank near the National Museum. You enter a courtyard ablaze with flower beds around a large central pool that reflects the image of the small graceful mosque at the far end. The beauty and quiet of the courtyard make it a favorite spot for students to study for their government examinations. Two slender minarets like white pencils frame the arched porch and high dome which has a row of windows around its base. These windows have the unusual feature of stained glass through which the light plays an ever-changing color pattern on the simple white marble floor and walls.

The courtyard is flanked by colonnades and a series of domed guest cells, each with its own fireplace and chimney. Over each doorway is a decorative panel of beautiful blue tiles. Here visiting scholars—and they were great travelers in the old days—could rest and study. Other mosques are older, larger, or more sacred, but few, if any, have the beauty and charm of this gem of Muslim architecture.

Across the street is the National Museum with a large shady courtyard filled with Greek and Roman sculptures. A restoration of the beautiful gateway of one of the Omayyad desert hunting lodges, Kasr al Kheir, faces the garden. This gateway and flanking towers had been found scattered into fifty thousand pieces, but they were carefully reassembled, a job that is a tribute to the archeologists' skill.

The museum concentrates on the Greek, Hellenistic, Roman, and Arab cultures. In addition to the well-arranged displays typical of any good museum, there are two rooms of unusual interest. One is a complete tomb-chamber transplanted from Palmyra, with its distinctive portrait sculpture decorating the burial niches. The other is a small synagogue from Dura Europos, a Palmyran outpost on the Euphrates.

This is unique in that the walls are covered with frescoes of Jewish Biblical scenes in gay, fresh colors. Dating from the middle of the third century A.D., the synagogue had scarcely been finished when a

The gardens of the Mosque of Sultan Suleyman I.

threat of war caused it to be filled with sand and included as a part of the strengthened city wall. There it remained forgotten and undamaged until discovered a few years ago and carefully removed to the museum.

On the other side of the city is the traditional Church of St. Paul, which is of doubtful merit. Even more doubtful is the site of St. Paul's conversion. It has been moved to various spots through the years to accommodate shifting tourist interest.

The new apartments and residences are creeping up the mountainside back of the city. From the Muhajereen Square, part way up the slope, you get a fine view of the city and the encircling gardens of the Ghuta. Perhaps one should go there first to study the plan of the city as it lies below. For a closer view, many of the big

At the Damascus International Fair.

hotels have roof terraces offering vantage points for picture taking.

Since 1954 Damascus has been host to an international fair. The large attractive park and the permanent buildings lie along the Barada River which reflects the gay colors and bright lights. About twenty-five major countries exhibit each year.

As the capital of the state, Damascus is also host to the embassies and consulates of the old and new nations. But much of the old glamour has departed from these now streamlined agencies. Formerly the *Kavass* ornamented the embassy doorways and preceded the ambassadors on all official visits. They were a colorful lot, dressed in baggy pants, contrasting sashes, shirts, and short heavily embroidered jackets of scarlets, blues, and greens. A red fez topped their impressive height and a long, curved sword added much to their swaggering dignity. Now, only the highest church dignitaries continue the custom of being preceded by a Kavass on all public appearances. A lot of colorful pageantry has given way to the drab sack suit and brief case of today's harried officials.

CHAPTER ELEVEN

The Beehive Village

THE MOST unique feature of the Syrian landscape north from Damascus is the "beehive" village. From Homs north to Aleppo, these villages cluster about ancient tells or dot the plains, occupying an area roughly thirty miles wide by one hundred and fifty miles long. The houses are built from red-brown clay on which they squat, and make an ideal shelter in a treeless land: cool in summer and warm in winter. Imagine scores of large brown cubes with a brown, pointed dome on each block. The early Italian merchants, coming to trade in Aleppo, gave them the name "beehive" because they looked like the familiar beehives of Italy. This term is still used even though the local hive for bees is a two foot cube made of mud.

The houses cluster together in a hit-and-miss jumble but usually leave bare a rough square of earth at some point for dancing. At the edge of the village there will be a similar smoothed square for threshing. There will be a guest house, two or three times larger than the dwellings, with a flat mud roof instead of a dome.

Also it is a poor village indeed that does not have its domed tomb of some saint. Probably the name of the saint and the story of his works have long been forgotten, but it is still a holy spot, where the young girls go to pray for a husband. Both the tomb and the guest house will be whitewashed to distinguish them from the red-brown houses.

The beehive houses are not only nicely adapted to their kind of rolling clay countryside, but are also easy to build. An old one may tumble down under the soaking rains, or a family may need more room. Then the man of the house picks a nearby hollow to use as a mixing pit. The girls carry water while the men and boys tread up a big puddle of sticky mud mixed with chopped straw. The women carry baskets of the mortar on their heads to a sunny spot where they tread the mud into simple wooden forms of bottomless boxes that hold two bricks at a time. When the bricks are firm enough to stand alone, the forms are slipped off them and refilled. The bricks measure 18 by 10 by 3 inches and look somewhat like our cement blocks. They dry quickly in the hot sun.

Beehive domes make a village.

In two or three weeks a busy family (all the relatives help in this housebuilding) can make the required four thousand bricks and they are ready to build. Again a nearby hollow is watered and trampled into mud. This mortar and the bricks are carried by the women and girls to the spot selected for the new house. A space twenty feet square is leveled off and marked with string. Then the walls begin to rise.

The men lay the bricks in a simple basket-weave bond, making a wall about thirty inches thick. Space is left for a doorway. When the walls are about three feet high the men begin corbelling, that is, they start filling in the corners, each course of brick hanging out a bit over the one below. In one corner a salt jar is buried. The salt is kept in it although no one seems to know why the custom persists. By the time the walls are ten feet high the bricks have so completely filled the corners that the opening is nearly round instead of square.

After that, the dome is easily built. Each circular course is laid a little smaller in diameter than the one beneath until the dome is complete. Then the women mix up more mud and straw and pat a smooth coating over the walls and dome, inside and out. Add a simple wooden doorframe and door, a couple of weeks' time to dry out, and all is ready for the family to move in. Of course every spring the women have to pat on another coat of mud to repair the damage done by the winter rains. With that yearly care the house will remain dry, but if neglected will soon crumble into the mud from which it was made.

In some of the very hot valleys a crude form of air conditioning is achieved. While the dome is being built, lengths of wood about four inches in diameter are built into the courses. The wooden plug is turned and twisted occasionally until the mud hardens. In summer the plugs are pulled out and you have a ventilated dome. Another variation in style around Hama is for the dome to be decorated with an occasional row of projecting stones.

Inside the house, the floor, a fifteen-foot square of hardened earth,

Inside a beehive house.

is covered with reed matting. The bedding, consisting of cotton quilts, is neatly stacked in one corner. A gaily painted wooden trunk for clothes stands in another corner. Bunches of dried peppers and bright raffia serving trays hang from the ceiling. On the wall opposite the door is a wooden shelf with a mirror over it. The mud bracket for the shelf will be scratched in geometrical designs and the hollows of the design filled with colored tin foil carefully saved from candies. On the shelf will be the family treasures, a comb and brush, old bottles, and a few cheap trinkets, souvenirs of trips to the nearby city.

Once away from the clay plains, in the mountains and in basalt hills along Syria's northern border, the houses are rectangular with flat roofs. The walls are of roughly cut stone with door and window openings. Ceilings are made by putting small cottonwood poles close together. These are often painted in gay, decorative patterns. On top of the poles brush is tramped down to a compact cover about a foot thick. Next an eight-inch-thick layer of clay is spread and rolled smooth.

After a heavy rain the owner goes over his roof with a stone roller to squeeze the water out of the clay before it has time to seep down to the rooms below. Perhaps this explains why most ancient temples have lost their columns: they make such good rollers.

In both types of houses fireplaces are a rarity, usually only found in the village guest house. Baking is done in small, conical clay ovens shared by a number of families. Fuel is scarce and anything burnable, such as straw, cotton stalks, or dung mixed with chopped straw and patted into flat cakes, is carefully saved.

An unleavened bread is a staple of Arab diet. Girls build a quick hot fire of straw or twigs in the oven. Coarse wheat dough is pounded

A village girl baking bread.

into large thin pancakes. The baker, wearing a padded mitten, slaps the pancake against the inside of the oven. Heat quickly bakes the bread and the baker deftly catches it as it falls from the oven wall. The result is a bread looking like a piece of grey chamois but tasting delicious. A triangular piece crimped between two fingers and the thumb makes an ideal spoon to scoop gravy or stews.

Actually the village families spend little time in their houses unless the weather is cold or rainy. The men and women get up at dawn, sip a glass of tea, and go to the fields to work until ten o'clock. Then they drink more tea with some bread, goat cheese, and fruit or vegetables if in season. After this "brunch" they continue working until it gets too hot, about two or three in the afternoon.

Back in the village the women draw water from the village well and prepare a simple dinner. Cracked wheat, called *bourghul,* is the main food. In the winter it is eaten as a thick gruel, with scoops of bread for a spoon. In the spring, the bourghul is soaked until soft, drained, and combined with chopped tomatoes, peppers, onions, garlic, and any other greenstuff available. Mixed with olive oil and seasoned, it becomes a salad called *tabbouli,* a sure sign that spring has arrived. Meat is a rarity in the villager's diet. On festivals or feast days the meat will be roasted mutton or goat meat. Camel meat is also eaten but more often by the Bedouins than the villagers.

Electricity has not reached many of the villages. One energetic young landowner, fresh from an American agricultural college, did rebuild his village on concrete floors. He gave the beehives a permanent coating of cement, piped in water, and put in an electric plant for lights, to the astonishment of the neighboring villages. The electric lights were something to enjoy and boast about. But the women refused to use the piped water. They could not get any gossip out of a faucet so they trooped daily to the well with their water cans balanced on their heads.

Not all landlords are so progressive. That is Syria's major problem. All too much of the land is owned by wealthy landlords who manage their farms on a feudal system. The owner supplies the seeds, tools, and a few draft animals. Oxen still draw the bent-stick plow shod with an iron tip, used in Biblical times. Much of the land is still worked in long narrow strips as was done in the Middle Ages. Too often the owner takes an excessive share of the crops.

A few villages are cooperatively owned and are buying tractors, but they still use the feudal method of strip farming. The government is now endeavoring to redistribute the lands to individual farmers who will till their own acres; but the plan, naturally, is meeting much opposition from the wealthy landlords who like to be known as a five-, ten-, or a fifty-village landlord.

Most of the villages are isolated by the sticky mud during the winter. Life is dull with only the village radio in the guest house as a contact with the outside world. By spring, however, they will find some excuse to make merry and dance the debke. It is an ancient dance handed down from the Phoenicians. In Arab villages, only the men form a conga line, to hold hands and shuffle and stamp intricate steps. They are led by a dance master waving a bright handkerchief. To Western eyes, the slow crablike steps seem monotonous, but not to an Arab. Each village is convinced that it does a more intricate, subtle dance than any other village. The women sit on the sidelines and clap their hands or give out shrill Indian war whoops by patting their mouths.

When there is a wedding, the whole village takes part in the entertainment of the guests. In the village square a long canvas awning is put up, under which are placed rugs and cushions for the village owner, his honored guests, and the headmen from surrounding villages. The rest of the guests sit on the ground in the shade and smoke the bubble pipes passed to each guest in turn.

A band consisting usually of a drummer and a flutist marches out to escort groups of guests into the village. The groom welcomes all the guests as they straggle in across the fields, while the bride waits in her parents' home to receive the gifts. The marriage ceremony has actually taken place three days before, when male representatives of both families met at the house of the imam (religious leader) to sign the contract and before witnesses pay the dowry agreed on by the bride's family. It is a joyous occasion when brother and sister marry sister and brother, for then no dowry is demanded. That happy circumstance leaves all the more money for the wedding feast which may go on for days.

The groom and the landlord provide sheep and rice for the feasting. The guests bring gifts, usually lengths of gaily colored dress silks or cottons, or perhaps a mirror or some sweets. All the gifts are carefully taped to wooden tables, to be carried later around the village so that everyone can see them.

The band now plays for the guests to dance the debke. As one lot drops out exhausted, another group of dancers will take their place,

Men about to dance the debke.

to go on and on. There will be horseraces in the fields adjoining the village and some footraces by the youngsters.

Toward evening huge trays, six feet in diameter, heaped with rice and chunks of mutton, with gravy and hot peppers floating around the rim, are placed before the guests. A servant brings a pitcher of water and a towel. Hands are ceremoniously washed and then dipped into the mound of food, which disappears like magic.

At dusk the groom is escorted by the men to the bride's door. She has been busy doing the traditional wailing at having to part from her parents. Then, heavily veiled and wearing a long velvet dress even in summer, she is put on the back of a horse and led to the groom's house where they are both laughingly shoved through the door by their friends.

The villagers go back to the square for more eating, dancing, and perhaps for some unorthodox drinking of arak. Lanterns are lit and the celebration goes on far into the night until everyone drops from exhaustion. The feasting and dancing will go on for days until the food and drink run out, along with the groom's money.

CHAPTER TWELVE

Aleppo, the Commercial Capital

ALEPPO has been the goal of weary caravans from India and China for hundreds of years. As host to merchants and drovers as well as to invaders and the tribesmen of the desert, the city has been the commercial mecca of the Middle East. Down through recorded history it has been the terminal where merchandise from the East has been diverted to markets of the world lying to the north, west, and south. Aleppo is still the commercial capital and largest city in Syria with over four hundred fifty thousand citizens and a potential market of a million and a half customers.

Nor has the character of the city changed much during the centuries. The modern section, with its new apartment houses, looks much like any Mediterranean city. But as a whole it is still a medieval city, its houses and shops clustered in tight, haphazard confusion around the massive Citadel, sitting on its tell like an inverted bowl on a plate. The narrow, twisting streets present blank walls that hide from the passer-by beautiful inner courtyards and handsome houses.

Architecturally it also has its distinctive character. Built of the native stone on which the city rests, it has developed a style of its

Aleppo from the air, showing the Citadel and the Zakariah Mosque.

own—a nice blending of Turkish and Arabic traditions that have produced a pleasing harmony of style without losing strength of character. In the streets of houses in the old quarters latticed wooden balconies still project in saw-toothed rows from the second stories. Built of wood in intricate patterns suggesting tile work, they provide the women of the house an ideal vantage point from which to watch, with all modesty, the traffic in the streets below.

For centuries Aleppo was surrounded by protective walls. Bits and pieces still remain and also a few of the gates. Outside the walls, fruit orchards stretched for miles, and in the spring, made the city the center of a huge pink, white, and green Oriental carpet. Diversion of the water of the Quate River into Turkey in 1926 marked the end of most of the orchards. Now Aleppo, at great cost, pumps and filters her water from the Euphrates some sixty miles away, and apartments and factories have replaced the colorful gardens.

Today visitors can get their most comprehensive view of the city

Old house with Turkish balconies.

from the throne room of the Citadel. The monotony of the square-roofed houses is broken by the gleaming white domes of mosques further accented by the shafts of minarets in a variety of styles representing the long and varied history of Islam. They are of all styles:

Aleppo's vaulted souks.

converted square Byzantine bell towers, tall Turkish pencil-like shafts with sharp conical caps, and Arab columns with decorative balconies and rounded caps.

The older core of the city is being surrounded by modern shops, apartments, textile factories, and all the supplementary services of a big city such as warehouses, cotton gins, slaughterhouses, and the inevitable acres of cemeteries.

Equal to the Citadel in interest to the tourist are Aleppo's famed souks, about eighteen miles of narrow streets and little shops. Most of the shops are crowded into a complex of streets covered by stone vaulted roofs dating from the thirteenth century. Cool in summer and warm in winter, the streets are dimly lighted by pierced domes over the street intersections. Bedouins, townsmen, merchants, donkeys, bicycles, carts, and tourists jostle each other in the crowded passageways.

Aleppo's souks with their stone roofs have survived while the souks of Damascus, Istanbul, Cairo, and other cities have been burned and then modernized. The souks of Aleppo are a National Trust and not to be changed.

The different crafts are grouped together by streets according to the medieval guild-system. A street of tinsmiths leads to the rope merchants or to the leather workers. One dim tunnel is brightened with thousands of the popular red leather slippers, another with shop after shop of gay silks or piles of brilliant yarns.

The Spice Street, once the center of the spice trade to Europe, is nearly two miles long. It still has a spice market but the remainder of the street is a succession of shops selling foods, cereals, nuts, and candies. At the end near the Citadel are products older than the spice trade: camel saddles and bridles, long rolls of black felt for Bedouin tents, and gaily painted little dower chests for the desert bride.

The shops are still organized on the medieval guild system, with a guild master for each craft. The guild master arbitrates all disputes between buyer and seller and checks to see that the products are up to standard.

Tucked away in this maze of souks are two mosques, a "Turkish" bathhouse, and, for good measure, a saint's tomb. There are also six large *khans* left from the many built to house the foreign merchants who were licensed to trade with the Ottoman Empire. The khans consist of storerooms built around a large open square that was entered through a doorway large enough for drays to bring in their loads of merchandise. The gateway, often handsomely decorated, can be closed by a heavy, iron-covered door.

Above the storerooms are the living quarters of the merchants or factors, their families, and clerks. Some of the European families have lived in their khans for centuries. The Marcopoli family has represented Italian interests for generations and is descended from Marco Polo. The Pochés came from Austria one hundred fifty years ago and still live in the five-hundred-year-old Venetian Khan.

Up until the First World War they were carefully locked in each night by the suspicious Turkish authorities. Consequently the families developed a social life of their own, visiting each other across the roofs of the souks. The custom still prevails and if you are fortunate enough to be invited to a roof-garden party under the light of a summer moon, you will be transported to the magic world of Harun-el-Rashid, remote, mysterious, and utterly fascinating.

The khans overlook the great Zakariah Mosque which is similar to the Great Mosque at Damascus. It also was originally a Byzantine church and the square bell tower, raised as a minaret and beautifully decorated with Arab arches, is a landmark in the city. The colonnaded courtyard is pleasing in its simplicity. The prayer room allegedly contains the tomb of Zakarias, father of John the Baptist. As with Damascus, the great mosque at Aleppo has been burned and restored several times.

Unfortunately the old mosques and charming minarets are rapidly becoming hidden by office and apartment buildings. Modern cubes of stone and concrete are forming a new, harsh skyline. The miles of open-street souks, unlike the covered souks of the thirteenth century, are also affected and many are having modern fronts installed with signs in neon lights. The old yellow glow of the city at night is rapidly changing to the harsh reds, greens, and blues of neon tubing spelling out "progress."

The older sections of the city are best explored on foot with a guide, unless you enjoy getting lost in a maze of rambling streets. The northeast, Christian section has particular interest because it contains churches representing the various Eastern sects. The Armenian Orthodox church has a lovely baptismal font dating from Byzantine times. Many of the churches have fine old paintings or icons. In the same quarter are several beautiful houses hidden behind blank walls and dating from the seventeenth century. Once through the tunnel-like doorways, you step into shaded gardens with fountains that refresh the rooms fronting on them. Some of the courtyard walls are decorated with arabesque designs in stone. Many rooms still have the elaborately decorated ceilings characteristic of the period, like those in the Azam palaces.

Certainly one should visit the National Museum of North Syria, just off the Rue Baron. The handsome new building houses the archaeological finds of the pre-classical periods, including such peoples as the Sumerians, Hittites, Assyrians, and Phoenicians. A visit to the museum makes for a better understanding and appreciation of both the antiquity of the land and its rich cultural heritage.

Aleppo having played host to countless caravans during the centuries is a friendly city. There are more smiles and fewer beggars than elsewhere. A number of first-class hotels are available to the visitor. The most famous, The Baron, has that aura of personality acquired by only a few hotels about the world. Its host is a cultivated and gracious Armenian, Krikor Mazlumian. His guest book contains the names of many of the world's great, from royalty and celebrities to the "top brass" of two wars. T. E. Lawrence and

Agatha Christie have signed it, as have Sir Leonard Woolley and many others. During the long summer months you can sit on the terrace and watch the world go by as one used to do at Shepheard's in Cairo.

In her familiar role of host, Aleppo has, since 1955, promoted an annual Cotton Festival. For a three-day long weekend in the latter part of September, the minister of agriculture and a crowd of public officials, members of Aleppo's chamber of commerce, delegates from other chambers, and representatives of foreign countries gather on a Thursday evening in a huge tent set up for the occasion. The guests are welcomed by a high dignitary, and verses are read from the Koran, blessing the festival and all the guests. The Mohaffez and others make the usual happy-to-be-here speeches.

The sweetmeat vendor pushes his wares along an Aleppo street.

Next day there is a parade of all civic organizations with their elaborate floats. A Cotton Queen reigns over the contests of dancing teams of both men and women from rival villages around Aleppo. The gorgeous costumes of the women recreate scenes from medieval pageantry.

Needless to say there are exhibits by foreign firms concerned with the cotton industry. But they do not interfere with the more important business of eating one's way through huge banquets. In addition, villages that raise cotton take turns to play host to selected guests, who are stuffed into happy torpor. Everyone has a good time in the best tradition of harvest festivals the world over.

Aleppo's rapid growth causes dislocations of traffic that are unexpected. New streets are opened only to be blocked by piles of stone and sand as new buildings rise alongside. The streets are more crowded than ever with pedestrians, carriages, bicycles, donkeys, cars, trams, buses, and trucks. Only cars, buses, and trucks are required to obey traffic laws; the rest of the traffic swoops and darts on whim, a constant threat to life and limb. Driving a car in Aleppo is a frustrating, nerve-racking experience, particularly in the older sections. There is one comfort, however. If you get your car wedged into an impossible tangle of pushcarts, donkeys, pedestrians, and piles of merchandise, you can count on the whole group of bystanders to swarm good-naturedly to the rescue. Amid indescribable commotion they shout, grunt, push, haul, and lift until a path magically appears ahead of you. You shout, "Thank you, thank you!" and the crowd, proud of its English, replies, "Very much, very much!" and happily waves you on your way.

CHAPTER THIRTEEN

Towns Living and Dead

SYRIA has been the home of so many different peoples through her many centuries of history that her land is covered with old towns, monuments, and lonely tombs. They offer the visitor a wide choice of sites to visit according to his interests—archaeological, architectural, or religious. There are over one hundred deserted towns in the rocky hills and narrow valleys between Aleppo and the sea alone. Many of these towns were monastic retreats for the numerous divergent groups of the early Christian centuries.

The best known of the monastic towns is Deir Sam'an or Telanassos. During the first to fourth centuries A.D., it became a popular retreat for pious monks as well as for less pious refugees from debts or army service.

Its three-story hostels, built of stone, are surprisingly modern in design. We think our motels, which provide space close to the sleeping quarters, for the automobile, are a new idea. Deir Sam'an hostels provided rows of mangers and hitching rings for the donkeys and camels, "compact" transport of those years.

Besides the hostels there are several churches and shops. From the largest hostel a raised causeway of big stones leads to a half-circular paved terrace facing tombs cut into the rock hillside. Here the processions formed to go on the "sacred way" to a sharp spur of rock jutting out over the valley below. On top of the spur, evidently a sacred "high place" of antiquity, services were held. It was to this high place that Saint Simeon brought added fame in the early fifth century.

Saint Simeon, born about A.D. 386, dedicated himself to a life of piety. Soon his reputation for extreme self-punishment increased his fame for piety but won for him the displeasure of his less ascetic brethren. Asked to leave the community at Deir Sam'an, he finally took refuge on top of a column on the peak of a rocky spur above the community, now called Qal'at Sam'an.

His column was sixty feet high with a six foot square capital on which he chained himself for the last forty years of his life. Since he dressed only in a goatskin loin cloth and a leather cap, it is a miracle that he survived even a year. Anyone who has faced the bitterly cold winter winds blowing off the snow-covered Amanus Mountains just across the valley, or the blistering heat of the long summer, can only marvel at his endurance. Sitting on top of his pillar as a retreat from the world, he became an object of great interest to the pious public. Pilgrims came from as far away as England, France, and Spain to visit the holy man. The pope at Rome sent an envoy to check on his orthodoxy. Twice a day he preached to the crowds gathered below him and he is reputed to have made thousands of converts. Nor did he hesitate to advise kings and emperors on how to rule their states.

When Saint Simeon died in A.D. 459, his body was placed in a lead coffin at the foot of his column, but an armed force from Antioch removed the coffin to that city as a money-making pilgrim attraction. During the years of turmoil following the Muslim conquest all traces of the saint's resting place were lost.

Some years after his death a basilica or church, planned in the

*All that remains of
Saint Simeon's pillar.*

form of a Greek cross of four arms of equal length, was built around
the sacred pillar. Pious visitors have chipped souvenirs off the pillar
until only an egg-shaped remnant six feet high is left.

A small square baptistry at the other end of the spur from the
church blocks the "sacred way" up the hillside. Inside the building

is a large sunken baptismal tank with steps and doors at either end to speed the immersion of the thousands of pilgrims. Between the baptistry and the basilica one can still trace the foundations of the shops that sold refreshments and holy souvenirs.

Beside this dead monastic city, there are many others that once played even more exciting roles in history. There is, for instance, the Seleucid city of Cyrrhus, Nebi Uri, north of Aleppo close to the Turkish border. It was an important defense point against invaders from the north and east and became the administrative center for a succession of conquerors. The most striking monument near by is the tomb of Uriah the Hittite. The hexagonal stone tower and pyramidal roof can be seen on the horizon long before reaching it. It is said to mark the spot where Uriah fell in battle after King David, attracted to Uriah's wife, Bathsheba, sent Uriah to the battle front to be killed. The tower now contains a tomb of an unknown Muslim saint, but the romantic story of Uriah is too appealing to be forgotten.

Southwest of Aleppo on the road to Idlib, famous for its glassware,

The Basilica of Saint Simeon.

The tomb of Uriah, the Hittite.

one passes the remains of many buildings and tombs dating from various periods and in equally various degrees of ruin. One such complex is the once large city of Bara, a good example of the scores of "ghost towns" one sees throughout northern Syria. The best-preserved buildings are a number of large square tombs with finely carved decorative bands around the walls. But most striking are a series of smaller square tombs capped with tall pyramidal roofs dating from the fifth and sixth centuries of the Christian era.

In contrast to Bara, there is very little visible of the once important city of Apamea. Not old, as cities are reckoned in the Middle East, it was founded by Seleucus Nicator after the death of Alexander the Great in 323 B.C. The city was named in honor of Apamea, Seleucus's wife. The only ruin left of any size is the *Tycheon,* a small temple to the goddess of fortune. In the spring, when the once great city lies asleep under a tender green blanket of wheat, one should walk there warily. The fields are infested with a variety of viper that, curiously, travels with the first third of its body and head raised for better vision: a most disconcerting sight to meet, unless you like snakes.

Many dead cities on the desert have little left to show their former importance. Raqqa, built on the bank of the bend of the Euphrates where it starts to turn southeasterly toward Iraq, was long an im-

A pyramidal tomb at Bara.

portant city on the caravan route. Haroun-al-Rashid and his court chose Raqqa as the summer capital to get away from the muggy heat of Baghdad.

Some eighteen miles southward on the desert the walls and towers of Resafa rise glittering in the sunlight. A small walled city, it is built of a local rock heavily flaked with mica. The glitter caused the Arabs to call it the "City of Gold."

Long a caravan stop on the way from the Euphrates to Palmyra, it is mentioned in the Bible as Rezeph. It was not until the fourth Christian century that it became a place of pilgrimage. Here a centurion officer was beheaded about A.D. 303 for refusing to give up his Christian faith. A little chapel on a knoll opposite the north gate of the city marks the spot of his martyrdom. The reputation of Saint Sergius, as he came to be known, started a flood of pilgrims coming to this holy spot. Renamed Sergiopolis, the town was enlarged and fortified with walls and flanking towers.

Sixty miles to the southwest lies Palmyra. However, it is more easily reached from Homs, driving eastward one hundred miles across the desert with the telegraph line of the Iraq Petroleum Company as guide.

Palmyra lies in a well-watered oasis just beyond the pass through the Djabel Sharki range of mountains. Once over the pass, the road winds through a narrow valley lined with stark square towers several stories high. These are the "tower tombs" of the ancient Palmyrenes, reminding one of the square bell towers of Italy. Each provided burial niches for as many as a hundred members of a family. A central stairway winds up the tower with square niches, tier on tier, on all four sides. Most of the square stone covers that closed the ends of the niches are now in museums or private collections, for they were decorated with sculptured portraits of the dead. These sculptures have a realism and warmth that once seen can be recognized anywhere.

Once through the Valley of the Tombs, the road leads down to the main avenue of the city, still lined with a great colonnade. The columns have brackets which originally held portrait busts of the prosperous merchants who were very proud of themselves. They loved to entertain lavishly and sent out invitations on baked clay with their portraits on one side and the mouth-watering menu on the other.

Roman society came to depend on Palmyra's agents and their well-organized caravans to provide Chinese silks, jade, and Indian incense, spices, ivory, pearls, and precious stones. The traders' profits were one hundred per cent and the wealthy families lived like the princely merchants of Venice of a later day. It was to Rome's interest to support and indulge the Palmyrenes, to give them Roman citizenship, and to make some of the princes senators.

But Odaenathus, prince of Palmyra, misjudging Rome's actual strength, boldly occupied the Roman provinces of Syria and Asia Minor. When he was murdered, his widow Zenobia carried on the

The street of the columns, Palmyra.

territorial expansion. Calling herself "Queen of the East," in A.D. 267, she declared Palmyra an independent kingdom.

Five years later the Roman Emperor Aurelian defeated the queen and her army at the Orontes River in Syria. Zenobia escaped to Palmyra where the city was soon under siege. After haughtily refusing Aurelian's terms of surrender, she slipped out of the city on a racing camel. She almost made good her escape, but was captured as she tugged desperately to free a boat to cross the Euphrates.

Aurelian took her and her children to Rome where, bound in golden chains, she graced his triumph. The streets and roof tops were lined with crowds eager to see the beautiful and famous queen. The emperor felt rather sheepish about the whole affair and sent a letter to the senate defending his warring on a woman. He claimed, and rightly, that Zenobia had provided the brains and courage behind the whole Palmyrene campaign.

Today the ruins of Palmyra, like golden bones on the open plain, make it hard to imagine the city as it once was, populated and pulsing with trade. To recapture the ancient spirit, it is helpful to go before dawn to the ruined seventeeth-century Arab castle on the mountainside above the city. There, crouched in the moat out of the blast of the icy desert wind, you can easily imagine Palmyra in all her glory, as the rising sun chases shadows through the columns and bathes their capitals in gold. Then Palmyra comes to life, awaking to the bustle of commerce and trade as the caravans march along her streets and out into the desert beyond the bordering palm trees.

But a visitor to Syria need not be interested only in dead cities, for there are many ancient cities still flourishing, with distinctive interest. One such is Hama, a conservative Muslim city where, until recently, the Christian women wore veils in public to escape recognition. It was once a great weaving center with five thousand looms banging twenty-four hours a day. It is said that Turkish toweling was first made here. Nestled in the deep river canyon, this city of one hundred thousand is hidden from the plain until you suddenly

Remains of the past dot the Syrian plains. The Hellenic Theater of Cyrrus, North Syria.

drop into the valley. The Orontes flowing through Hama turns huge water wheels called *noria*. The huge wheels, some of them eighty feet in diameter, are made of wood and are turned on wooden axles by the current of the river. The wooden cups on the wheels lift the water to aqueducts that distribute it to the houses and orchards. A comfortable hotel and extensive gardens face the largest of the water wheels and provide a delightful place to stop.

Another very old but bustling city is Homs, with a population of a quarter of a million people. It was called Emesa in Old Testament times. It is now the junction of the railways and highways to the other northern cities of Syria and is also an administration post for the long trans-Arabian pipeline from Iraq to the coast.

The towns to the north and east are of little interest architecturally or historically and the great area of the Jezire is closed to the tourist because of political unrest among the Kurdish settlers. But there are a number of cities along the coast that reward one's visit.

They are all of Phoenician origin, although no evidence of its

The Keylani Palace in Hama has its private noria, *or water wheel.*

origin exists at the big port city of Latakia. Since the loss of Iskanderun to Turkey, the port has been developed as Syria's major outlet to world trade. The harbor, protected by a long sea wall, provides modern loading docks where the tramp ships can pick up cotton and textiles for the Arab world. It is also the port that has given the name "Latakia" to the mild tobacco most American smokers prefer to have blended with their stronger Virginia tobacco. Latakia is a collection of attractive houses filled with bustling people. Resort hotels and restaurants make it a popular vacation spot. North of the city are beautiful stretches of white sand that provide ideal bathing beaches. The wooded mountains behind them are popular resort areas.

South of Latakia, the town of Banias has taken on new life after having slept through the years since the Crusaders left. It is now the end of the long pipeline that brings oil from northern Iraq. The Iraq Petroleum Company or I.P.C. as it is called locally, pumps the oil through underwater lines to the tankers lying a mile offshore. Back of the town a "tank farm" of huge storage tanks seems out of place because it looks so modern.

Three miles off the harbor lies the Island of Rouad, or Arwad. Much of the time it was a part of the Phoenician kingdom of Tortosa. The kidney-shaped island was walled and provided a safe harbor on its concave side. Today the visitor can scramble over the remnants of the old Phoenician walls and walk the crowded streets too narrow for any cart. The island is still the home port of the coast sailing fleet whose distinctive rigging permits the ships to maneuver the narrow Dardanelles into the Black Sea ports. It is also the home port of the sponge fishermen, who still dive as did the spongers of old, without the aid of any modern equipment.

Sailors on the island of Arwad.

CHAPTER FOURTEEN

Games and Recreation

IN A LAND largely desert, lacking forests, streams, and lakes, there are few recreation areas. Camping, fishing, hiking, and boating are impossible. Picnics are popular in early spring and late fall, but even then shady attractive spots are few and require long bus rides to get to them.

Organized games are popular among the young school people. The foreign schools have introduced basketball, soccer, volleyball, and softball. Inter-school rivalry is keen but distances and frontier restrictions make competition with schools of other countries difficult. All the larger cities have sports stadiums.

The teams that travel about representing their various countries are really professionals although they pretend to be amateurs. Athletic associations accept these conditions, for most Eastern countries send their teams abroad to build up national prestige.

Tennis, ping-pong, and track meets are especially popular because they offer the opportunity for "star" performances. The Middle Easterner's strong individualism makes him prefer games in which he can shine as an individual. "Teamwork" is an idea new to these lads and it takes a long time to build a sense of team loyalty.

Since independence, the young men of the Arab countries have become enthusiastic about physical fitness. Body-building and weight-lifting clubs are popular and numerous. Their members parade on every occasion, their chests proudly bearing the insignia of their clubs. Remember, however, that these boys are the privileged minority.

Most boys have to go to work at an early age, although the government is now trying to keep them in school longer. The average city youngster is too busy running errands, carrying coffee to the business offices and shops, shining shoes, or baby-sitting to have time for school or play.

In the villages, the slack seasons offer more time for fun. Boys play a simple form of soccer with a ball made of old rags. Foot races and wrestling take place in the cool evenings. Donkey races are great sport with most of the riders tossed off before they reach the finish line.

Little girls learn, at an early age, to be mothers' helpers. Like most

A game of softball.

girls they play with dolls. In the villages these are corn husks with a bit of a dress. The dolls are faceless in Muslim families, in accordance with Muhammed's warning against worshipping idols.

One game, called Crusader or Saladin, is played by men and boys. Two boys, called knights, are carried pickaback by two men called horses. The boys' hands and feet are tied so they won't fall off. A third boy is bound like a mummy and laid on the ground. He is the "castle wall." Both men are given wide leather belts and stand on either side of the castle wall. At a signal each starts hitting his opponent while at the same time trying to dodge the other's blows. The knights usually get the worst of it.

The major fun for the spectators is to listen to the lurid insults hurled by the "horses." Arabic lends itself to picturesque insults and the torrent of violent curses convulses the audience. The game ends with horses and riders falling from exhaustion and laughter onto the long-suffering castle wall.

Another game that must be older than Crusader is called, in Arabic, *Al-Minkala*. Stone slabs with rows of pits in them are found around most Roman army campsites. Two parallel rows of six shallow pits make the "board" with a storage pit at each end. In the villages the boys scoop out pits in the ground, and use pebbles or beans as counters. The game is to move the counters, one by one, so as to capture a pit full of the opponent's counters. Success lies in the player's ability in mental arithmetic to figure from which of his pits to make the first move in order to capture the most of his opponent's counters. The game is played with an incredible speed only possible to descendants of Phoenician traders. Under the name Kalah, the game is now available in toy and game stores.

Naturally it is the larger cities that have the greater variety of amusements. Parks offer a place to stroll during the day, past formal pools and gay flower beds laid out in geometrical designs. But at sundown all visitors must leave when guards lock the gates.

On Fridays and Sundays families go for a walk. Young boys and girls must do their strolling separately as is the custom in Spain and some other European countries. Boys and men will walk holding hands as do the girls. Although rather startling, the custom is simply a sign of friendship.

On summer evenings city families used to hire old-fashioned two-seated open carriages and clop, clop around the streets—now horse-drawn carriages are banned. Private automobiles are still a luxury of the official and wealthy classes and are rarely used for pleasure.

Upper-class families who can afford the expense like to spend their summers in cool mountain villages. Some of the villages favored with abundant springs and shade trees boast large hotels and casinos. Life here goes on much as it did at home. But most young people and their families have to get through the long summers as best they can. Afternoons are spent in long siestas. When the day begins to cool people stroll about the streets or go to the cinemas.

The movie houses vary in price and quality but do provide entertainment to all classes of society in the towns and cities. The larger cities will have a score or more of theaters that will be crowded every night. The Arabic films are usually made in Egypt and are wonderful to see. Every film, no matter what the plot, manages to crowd in every emotion from A to Z. It is like seeing an old "cliff-hanger" serial run off in one sitting. No one can complain about lack of action.

As everyone goes to the theaters three or four times a week, no matter how poor the programs, the operators are not forced to buy the best films. Consequently a lot of poor American, British, and French films are dumped on the Middle-Eastern market at attractively cheap rentals.

It is to be regretted because these poor films create a distorted image of the Western countries. For fear of curbing business freedom, we let films be exported at the expense of national reputations. Gangster pictures convince the viewer that American cities are blazing with gunfire all the time. West of Chicago, Indians and cowboys are shooting it out for possession of the range, and somewhere in between there is a large class of Americans who are all millionaires, spending their time driving madly about in big cars. British comedies, too subtle to be understood, confirm the Arab conviction that all Englishmen are mad. Such pictures are not only false but dangerous, for they foster both envy and hatred.

The small children love the puppet man. He travels from village to village and into the cities, carrying his puppets and folding stage on his back. Some of the shows are stories familiar to all youngsters, but he may also have his puppets act out bits of local history.

The time-honored storyteller, like the minstrels of medieval Europe, also goes about the country, an honored guest of the villages. In the cities he is often hired to entertain guests at a party. He will add jokes and riddles to his stories to keep the company amused.

Unfortunately, the radio is replacing the storyteller. Every village guest house has a radio blaring music and national propaganda. In the cities the noise is terrific. Each family enjoys its radio turned up to full volume.

In addition to the national radio stations, there is the powerful Cairo station calling for Arab unity under Egyptian leadership. The B.B.C. comes in from London with its clipped, unemotional news reports. The "Voice of America" broadcasts from the ship *Courier,* anchored off Cyprus. Russian stations are busily trying to jam all but their own programs that are used for propaganda purposes. The popularity of radio was inevitable. Perhaps it is a sign of progress and may eventually bring about better understanding of world problems. But the present use of radio for distorted propaganda rather than information makes it of questionable value.

Troops of boy scouts and girl scouts are popular. In a largely desert country there is obviously little opportunity to practice camping, tracking, and other types of woodcraft. Consequently, both groups spend much of their time learning military drill so that they can parade on every possible holiday occasion.

In spite of the limitations imposed by the nature of the land of Syria, Muslim youngsters grow up a happy lot, not expecting too much of the world around them. The boys are pampered by all the family but most of them become responsible citizens. Girls lead a more restricted life, limited to helping in household tasks and learning to cook and sew. If living in a town or city, the teen-age girl starts to wear a veil when out of her home, but she and her girl friends will go together to the cinema in the afternoon and chatter news and gossip like girls the world over.

Among men the universal center of recreation throughout Syria and the eastern Mediterranean is the coffeehouse. It is the Eastern counterpart of a club or of the English pub. In the larger cities the coffeehouse's customers tend to group together through mutual interests: guilds, trades, professions.

Turkish coffee was probably introduced to Turkey from Arabia during the reign of Suleiman the Magnificent (1520-66). The custom of serving it spread quickly so that it became the gesture of hospitality and friendship. The coffee is served in little cups holding six to eight teaspoons of liquid. One teaspoon of pulverized coffee and one of sugar are stirred into a cup of water, poured into a small coffee pot, and brought to a boil three times. Guests sip the scalding brew while chatting with their hosts.

Innumerable cups are consumed during the course of a day's business deals and social meetings. Many business transactions are completed in the coffeehouses. Then the parties relax with a game of tric-trac, our backgammon, while puffing on a *narghili*.

Turkish coffee leaves nearly a half-inch of sediment in the cup. Turned upside down, and allowed to drip and harden, it produces various patterns that are read by the coffeehouse fortuneteller, as are tea leaves in America and England. Where but in a coffeehouse can you complete a business deal, puff contentedly on a water pipe, enjoy stimulating cups of coffee, and have the future revealed to one? No wonder that the coffeehouse is so popular.

CHAPTER FIFTEEN

Transportation Then and Now

FOR CENTURIES the trade goods of Syria have been transported on the backs of animals. Even though the wheel had long been known, for lack of roads it had been proven impractical for anything but the narrow war chariots. Big and heavy loads were carried by the donkey and, after 1100 B.C., by the camel.

This beast proved to be an ideal carrier for long distances in desert lands. Shambling along on its broad padded feet, the camel looks ungainly but is capable of great stamina. It will plod along day after day, grunting and grumbling under a load of five hundred to six hundred pounds. Each beast is very fussy about just how much it will carry.

On the march, the camel can survive on a variety of desert shrubs no other animal would touch. Its big rubbery lips, like those of a clown, can nibble any brush, shrub, or thorn without injury. While there are records of forced marches of fifteen days without water, the camel does best if it can get water every three to four days. Furthermore it has a built-in water purifier that is a boon to its driver. The camel can drink from a fouled, slimy pool as long as it is wet. Her purifier will convert the fouled water into pure milk that sustains the driver.

The caravan routes southward to Egypt followed along the eastern slopes of mountain ranges and the edge of the desert. A coast route was impractical due to jutting promontories. The Phoenicians, like their neighbors the Greeks, were forced to grow as little city-states. All communication and commerce had to be carried on by ships. Early in the third century A.D. the Third Gallic Legion of Rome built a coastal road, but caravans shunned it because it was too open to ambush.

The story of the centuries-old caravan routes, the pilgrim roads, and the accounts of such early explorers as Henry Maundrell in the seventeenth century and Carsten Biebuhr and Dr. Richard Pococke in the eighteenth century, easily read in English, are full of fascinating details of camel transport. Huge caravans were usually broken up into units of one hundred and fifty to two hundred camels, spaced apart. It was found that larger numbers than these, on arriving at a watering place, caused confusion and delay.

The camel remained the only means of transport for long distances until the latter half of the nineteenth century when railroads were introduced to the Middle East. In 1863 a French company built the first road from Beirut over the mountains to Damascus. A service of diligence coaches cut the travel time from four days by horseback to thirteen hours. A European invention, the diligence was a top-heavy stagecoach with the body divided into three compartments. Driver and baggage were on the roof under a canvas hood, all giving the appearance of a combined stagecoach and covered wagon of pioneer days.

Soon this early bus system was extended from Damascus to the major cities of Syria. These bus roads made it easier to build railroads. In 1894 a narrow-gauge railroad from Beirut to Damascus replaced the diligences. It was quite an achievement, for the major pass through the Lebanons is five thousand feet high. Part of the way the little locomotive chugs on a cogwheel track. Extensive concrete sheds, looking like arched tunnels for a child's electric-train set, protect parts of the track from winter snowdrifts. In summer the sheds look oddly out of place in the bare, hot valleys.

By 1911 all the major cities of Syria were linked together by railroads. Unfortunately the roads were built by different companies under concessions bought from the Ottoman government, and the track gauge varies. Hence it is sometimes necessary to trans-ship the freight and passengers.

A standard-gauge line built from Aleppo southward to Hama and Homs turns westward to Tripoli on the coast. From Tripoli to Beirut the line winds along the beautiful Lebanese coast, reminding one of the famed Italian highway along the Gulf of Naples to Sorrento. The railroad provides sleeper service on an overnight run. A modern diesel-powered *automotriss* consisting of a coach with first-, second-, and third-class compartments and a baggage room supplements the old trains.

One other railroad venture had its start at the turn of the century when wily Sultan Abdul Hamid proposed to build a "Pilgrim Highway" to Mecca. All Muslim countries were invited to help finance the railroad. Abdul Hamid stressed the comfort and convenience for the pilgrims' travel without mentioning his own interest in being able to move his troops quickly to Arabia.

Work was started on the "Pilgrim Railroad" from Damascus to Medina in 1900 and finished eight years later. The pilgrims were able to travel in comfort for a few years until the outbreak of the First World War. It was this railway line that was raided and hopelessly damaged by Arab marauders led and financed by British officers. The campaign has been dramatized until it symbolizes the defeat of Turkish troops and the liberation of Arabia. The governments of Saudi Arabia and Jordan are now proposing to repair the line and reopen rail service between Medina and the Jordanian port of Aqaba, with access to the Red Sea.

In the 1890's Kaiser Wilhelm of Germany was dreaming of a Berlin-to-Baghdad railroad that would give German merchants quick access to the Persian Gulf and Far-Eastern markets. The scheme had the added importance that it would point an economic pistol at British interests in India and the Far East. The Kaiser and the Sultan saw eye to eye, and a German company was granted a concession to build the road in 1898.

Actual construction was slow. The route through the Taurus Mountains was particularly rugged. German engineers found, as had the French earlier, that wooden railroad ties were an irresistible temptation in a virtually treeless land. On cold winter nights the ties would disappear as fast as they were laid and Bedouin campfires

The Damascus station of the "Pilgrim Railroad."

twinkling in the night betrayed their fate. At great expense, metal ties made of ten-inch channel iron were substituted. The channel iron was laid edges down and splayed at the ends so as to grip the ground firmly.

Built in sections, the railroad was pushed from central Turkey through the mountains to the Euphrates River. A branch line connected with Aleppo. But there were still gaps in the line when war broke out in 1914. In particular, the gaps in the line from Constantinople were to embarrass the formation of the new Turkish Republic as it established its capital at Ankara.

The war also brought the gasoline truck to replace the donkey and camel as the burden carrier. Buses began to serve the villages and bring foodstuffs to the towns. Old diligence roads that had been badly neglected were repaired and extended.

When Syria came under French administration in 1920, the French engineers repaired old and built new roads—but largely for military purposes rather than to link the farmers to their markets.

The roads, fortunately, lie on the native rock and seldom have to cross soft ground. Still built by hand, they involve work that is laborious, slow, and inadequate for the heavy truck traffic. The abundant local rock is blasted into large chunks and delivered to the stretch of road to be built or repaired. Men appear with hammers and sit patiently breaking these large chunks of stone into pieces the size of a fist. These pieces they stack in a neat, smooth-topped rectangle, for they are paid by the cubic meter.

Next a gang roughly levels the roadbed, chipping off protruding points of rock. Masons appear with women helpers who carry baskets full of stone on their heads to the men who make a roadbed of carefully fitted stones laid one by one. Then a small gas-driven rock crusher grinds up the softer rock into a coarse powder that is wetted and rolled, by a lightweight steam-roller, into the stone bed as a binder. When this has been rolled to a satisfactory smoothness, a thin, all too thin, layer of asphalt is spread, apparently to keep the dust down rather than to protect the surface of the road. Very soon it becomes broken and pitted again.

Many of the major modern roads lie atop old Roman ones. Their skillful construction should have provided inspiration and guidance to the modern builder. A short distance from Aleppo there is still a mile and a half of the Roman road that once ran from the port of Antioch to Aleppo. The road consists of large blocks of cut stone varying in size but approximately twenty inches thick and all fitted closely together. After the chariots ceased to rumble over it, the road was used by camel caravans for more than a thousand years. The camel, very fussy about where he places his feet, always stepped daintily in the center of each block. Depressions in each stone show today where his pads were put.

Between the two World Wars trucks took much of the freight business away from the railroads, as they have in many other countries. Large buses haul passengers and an incredible variety of packages and baskets to villages and towns. Often sheep and turkeys plus a few extra children and bundles are tied on the roof. But no one minds the discomfort; the bus is faster than a donkey and a lot more fun.

For longer journeys, the regularly scheduled trips of large, eight-seat automobiles, called *services,* are preferred over buses. One can book a particular seat on a definite run by writing one's name on a seating chart. These cars are fast, often frighteningly so, and the trip is far from comfortable. The passengers are bounced and jostled as the drivers casually tear along the pitted and rutted roads.

It is often a relief to take off across the desert, usually smoother than the pitted highways, and drive by compass to your destination. The Nairn Transport Company has proven the value of the desert route by running scheduled trips from Damascus to Baghdad. They began the service before the Second World War with open cars and a lot of faith; now they run air-conditioned buses equipped with refrigerated foods and rest rooms. The larger part of the five hundred mile trip is made at night to avoid the desert heat. Leaving Damascus in the late afternoon, they roll into Baghdad fourteen hours later.

In 1946 the Mezze airport at Damascus became an international port. Runways were lengthened and widened, modern lighting and radio-control systems were installed. An attractive modern building with lounge, offices, and restaurant completes the equipment. Other airfields at Aleppo, Latakia, Deir-ez-Zor, and Qomishli are smaller fields designed to take care of domestic flights. The last two fields give the farmers of the northeast Jezire quick contact with the commercial centers of Aleppo and Damascus. The Syrian National Airways serves these airports and those of the surrounding countries. Neither Syria nor her neighbors attempt to compete with the big international airlines. Most of these lines serve Syria and Lebanon, proving once again that this region is a crossroads of the world's modern caravans.

A scale model of the new and greatly enlarged international airport in Damascus.

CHAPTER SIXTEEN

Syria and Her Neighbors

SYRIAN INDEPENDENCE brought with it a host of responsibilities, some foreseen and some unexpected. The feeling of Arab unity with neighbors sharing a common language, Arabic, and a common religion, Islam, began to cool under regional interests. Nationalistic ambitions in the regions began to separate the new nations: republics against monarchies, advanced cultures over underdeveloped peoples, and oil-wealthy countries envied by the "have-not" nations.

In the new pride of independence there was a natural repudiation of all advice or influence from the former imperial nations. The United States, which had enjoyed a long and favored position in Middle Eastern affairs from the arrival of the first missionaries in the 1820's, now found itself suspect from its association with colonial countries such as France and England.

Furthermore, the centuries of oppression under the Turks and years of repression under the French mandate had offered little experience in administration. It took time to adjust from being always *against* imposed policies to planning new policies *for* national progress. Yet the needs were great and the national leaders tackled

137

the basic problems of education, irrigation, industrialization, and land redistribution with vigor if not always with wisdom.

It was to be expected that the political parties would lean toward socialism in an endeavor to close the gap between the very rich and the great mass of the very poor. The Ba'ath Party, which had shown most consistent strength in politics, holds socialism, freedom, and Arab unity as its major objectives. It is opposed by the religiously oriented Muslim Brotherhood Party.

Underneath political phrasing is the basic need for land reform in an agricultural country. The farmer's income and ultimately the national income is dependent upon breaking up the feudal system of tenant farmers. At the same time the small farmer must be helped with machines, fertilizers, irrigation, and scientific advice in order to make his land productive.

The chamber of deputies under President Shukri el Quwatly started out bravely. Syria, already a member of the United Nations by invitation, joined the Arab League and took an active interest in world affairs. But the domestic path was rough. For a republic to perform successfully, it requires an educated, alert body of citizens aware of both domestic and foreign affairs. This Syria did not have. Nor did she and the other new Arab nations get much understanding or help from the Western democracies.

Western diplomacy was still confused by a myth that had grown after World War I. The exploits of Colonel T. E. Lawrence and his desert Arab legions, publicized in newspapers, books, and on lecture platforms, were followed by extravagant motion pictures such as *The Sheik* and its successors. Handsome Rudolph Valentino fixed the myth on western minds that the desert Arabs were noble, trustworthy, and "good." Fortunately, the "sons of the desert" were far enough away from Western eyes to maintain that image.

On the other hand, the Western diplomats were in contact with the young city Arabs, usually graduates of western schools, and were convinced that they were critical, impatient, and not to be trusted

Syria's Parliament chambers.

politically. In the language of the T.V. screen, they were the "bad guys." The tragic consequences of this myth were that arms, help, and loans were denied when most needed, forcing the young states to turn to the Iron-Curtain nations for arms and money denied by the West.

Nor did the rising power of the Zionist Party in Palestine help the political frustrations in the Middle East. The British administrators in Palestine were caught in a hopeless conflict of the promises of the vague Balfour Declaration, which said: "His Majesty's Government view with favor the establishment in Palestine of a national home for the Jewish people and will use their best endeavors to facilitate the carrying out of this objective, *it being clearly understood that nothing shall be done which may prejudice the civil and religious rights of non-Jewish communities in Palestine,* or the rights and political status enjoyed by Jews in any other country." On the other hand was Britain's promise of Arab independence in return for help against the Central Powers in the First World War.

The Zionist leaders interpreted the declaration as an invitation to create a Jewish political state. When Britain, alarmed at the mass migration into little Palestine, closed the borders, an underground Zionist army made terrorist attacks on the British forces and Arab villages. In disgust at their unsuccessful attempts at compromise solutions the British administration dumped the problem in the United Nations' lap and pulled out the last of their forces on May 14, 1948. Neither Britain nor the United Nations provided for an interim administration to prevent chaos.

The Zionist leaders proclaimed the new State of Israel. President Truman hastened to be the first to recognize the new state. To the Arabs this was a stab in the back by America, their old and trusted friend.

Two great branches of the Semitic race who had lived amiably together for more than three thousand years, now flew at each others' throats. Armies from the Arab states attacked the Israeli forces, but Arab individualism again plagued their attempt to carry on a successful war. There was no commander-in-chief over the Arab national armies. Operations were independent and each failed to support the other at crucial moments. The only fighting force capable of matching the Jewish veterans of the World War was the British-trained Arab Legion of Jordan. They occupied the territory west of the Jordan River coveted by King Abdullah and held the old city of Jerusalem. King Abdullah arranged a separate truce that left him holding that territory and half of Jerusalem.

During the first seven months of 1949, United Nations representatives negotiated armistice agreements between the warring countries and on the map drew a hasty line of demarcation between Israel and the Arab states. This armistice boundary line often divided villages and parted the farmer from his land and the village from its water supply. Consequently there have been and will continue to be raids and border incidents until a realistic boundary line is established and some solution of the present involved impasse is found.

Over nine hundred thousand Arab refugees fled to Egypt, Syria, Lebanon, and Jordan, the latter keeping the greatest share. None of these states is sufficiently industrialized nor has sufficient farmland to absorb all the refugees into their economy. The refugees exist by a dole from the United Nations through UNRRA, through help from private Christian agencies, and on what aid the host countries can contribute from their limited resources. The politicians refuse to accept Israel as an accomplished fact and consequently have done little to face up to the realities of the refugee problem.

The unsatisfactory ending of hostilities led to repercussions in all the Arab states. The Arab League declared a general boycott of all Israeli goods. In Egypt, the shocking disclosures of corruption and betrayal in high places led to the exile of King Farouk and the rise of Abdul Nasser as leader with visions of Egypt heading a union of all Arab states.

In Syria, the old human desire for a scapegoat to blame for the loss of national honor and dignity in the Israeli conflict led to a series of *coups d'état* from 1949 to 1953 when ambitious leaders overthrew constitutional government.

In December 1949, Brigadier Adib Shishakly headed a successful coup. He came from a prominent family in conservative Hama and was opposed to any land reforms, but he did much to stop profiteering and corruption among merchants and landowners. He showed admirable courage in visiting the dissatisfied commercial cities of northern Syria, but lacked clear-thinking, administrative ability. Again dissatisfied factions in the army forced him to flee to Switzerland. Constitutional government was restored in the middle of March, 1954.

All of this political confusion provided the Communist Party an opportunity to flood the country with cheap books and pamphlets promoting their beliefs. Agents worked among the various unhappy minority groups and also made big promises of land reform to the Arab tenant farmers.

The situation got so bad that the more responsible leaders turned to Egypt for moral support. For years the Egyptian radio had been screaming for Arab unity. In 1955 the armed forces of the two countries were placed under a unified command, to be followed by cultural and economic agreements in 1957. On the first of February, 1958, the two countries joined to form the United Arab Republic.

In the meantime a number of events had occurred to shake both the Arab and Western world. After riots and bloodshed, British troops were withdrawn from the Suez Canal zone in 1956. The attempt to enlist Arab support in the so-called Baghdad Pact to form an anti-Communist curtain along Russia's southern border failed when Syria and Egypt refused to join.

That same year the United States and Britain turned down Egypt's request for funds to build a high dam on the Nile River. As a result, President Nasser nationalized the Suez Canal for needed revenues and turned to Russia for engineering and financial help to build the dam. France and England were furious and predicted hopeless confusion. But to the surprise of all parties concerned, the Egyptians not only operated the canal successfully but also improved its facilities.

Following the nationalization of the canal, Israel, France, and Britain later staged an ill-advised attack on Port Said and the canal in October and November of 1956. Many lives were lost in the bombing and the canal was blocked for six months with sunken ships. British and French nationals were expelled from both Syria and Egypt. World-wide indignation and quick United Nations' action forced an armistice and then an uneasy truce under United Nations' supervision. Eventually all claims for war damage were satisfied on both sides.

After the United Arab Republic had been organized, the continual tirades of the Egyptian radio against the Baghdad Pact bore fruit in the July, 1958, revolution in Iraq, when the Hashemite royal family was wiped out. Repercussions led to disorders in Lebanon and Jordan. American troops were asked to come into Lebanon and British troops into Jordan. Within the year the foreign troops withdrew without any unhappy incidents and conditions became normal in both countries.

The union of Syria and Egypt strengthened the front against communism and stabilized Syrian economy. But the U.A.R. Northern Region, as Syria was called, was plagued with a series of droughts and scanty harvests. Business was slack; the merchants felt that they were being over-taxed; the large landowners resented President Nasser's proposed land reforms; the army officers resented being under Egyptian high command. Nor were the Syrian deputies happy about their lack of influence in the dual government.

Finally on September 28, 1961, a small group of army officers staged a *coup d'état*. President Nasser refused to strike back at Syria and withdrew his Egyptian troops. He is said to have been lukewarm to the idea of union from the beginning. In his radio address on October 5, 1961, he summed up the achievements of the union by saying: "What *matters* is that Syria should remain in existence." But the second star in the Egyptian flag, added after the union of 1958, remained there in the hope that the two countries would once again be united.

On her own again as the Syrian Arab Republic, she survived a series of cabinet crises and some ugly riots led by pro-Nasser partisans. Although it was the strongest politically in both Syria and Iraq, the Ba'ath Socialist Party was in a delicate position. While it was in favor of Arab unity, it resisted being absorbed into Nasser's National Front, one-party coalition. The Ba'ath Party, representing the influence of the growing intellectual middle class, was under constant pressure by Radio Cairo to do something about peasant concerns and land reforms. Radio Cairo blared daily appeals to the peasants, on the other hand, to demonstrate against the government and demand union with Egypt.

Nor was Syria unaffected by events in neighboring Iraq. Early in February, 1963, that equally strife-torn country had another revolt, this time under Abdel Salam Aref, who overthrew Brigadier Kassem and his government. Kassem had not fulfilled his promises of land reform, had done little to satisfy the Kurds' desire for greater autonomy or independence, and had shown an increasing tolerance of Soviet influence.

The Iraqi revolt sparked a military coup in Syria on March 8, 1963. The army was called out ostensibly to put down trouble in the Jezira, where the large Kurdish population in the northeast corner of Syria, like their fellow tribesmen in Iraq, were restless and unhappy. The Ba'ath Party supplied the political leadership. Socialistic theories were introduced a little at a time. Gradually the banks and insurance companies were nationalized, land allotments were proposed, and business enterprises were restricted by more and more regulations.

Having been on her own for only four years after the unfortunate experience of union with Egypt, Syria was open to a new proposal of federation with Iraq and Egypt, with the hope that Yemen, Kuwait, and Algeria would join later. A charter was drawn up with the intent to avoid the errors of the first union. Again, however, a great deal of the crucial power was left in the hands of the president, presumably Nasser.

Such a concentration of power in the hands of one person is traditional in the Middle East and might have succeeded because of its familiarity. But the presumed quiet acceptance by the people was not forthcoming. Their dissatisfaction was shown by a succession of coups d'état, averaging more than one a year. They resulted only in a reshuffling of old familiar political faces.

The federal idea finally died a still death as all countries became more engrossed with the Israeli problem. Restless, dissident Palestine refugees, impatient with two decades of inaction, formed bands of commandos called Fedayeen, and raided across Israeli borders. In June of 1967 the seething hatreds came to a boil in open war. The ensuing battles of the so-called Six-Day War resulted in victories for the Israeli armies. All Sinai was occupied east of the Suez Canal, as was the west bank of the Jordan River. Arab Jerusalem was taken, as were the strategic Golan Heights in Syria, overlooking Lake Tiberias.

The United States was blamed for the success of Israel. In bitter reaction Syria expelled all Americans from the country and closed her borders even to newsmen and diplomats.

Since then the UN has had a commission trying to maintain peace along the boundaries, with little success. The commando raids continued, Israel retaliated with bombings, swords rattled, and peace negotiations bogged down. Finally, in the fall of 1970, a cease-fire was achieved under UN auspices. It lasted, despite recriminations on the part of all countries concerned.

In the interim Gamal Abdel Nasser died suddenly of a heart attack. He was succeeded as president of Egypt by Anwar el-Sadat. As February 6, 1971 and the end of the cease-fire came, the world held its breath. Through the pressure exerted by the Big Four, Britain, France, Russia, and the United States, the fateful date passed and the negotiations continued. It may yet be possible to work out some satisfactory solution to this explosive problem.

CHAPTER SEVENTEEN

Syria Today and Tomorrow

As THE government of Syria was originally organized, and still is nominally, it is supposed to rest on the work of the chamber of deputies whose members represent the various districts of Syria. By secret ballot the deputies elect a President for a five-year term. His duties are more social than executive, for the real power lies in the council of ministers under the direction of the Prime Minister, designated by the President on show of party strength. In fact the government is organized like that of France and the President spends most of his time opening exhibits, greeting visiting dignitaries, and signing acts approved by the chamber of deputies.

Ten ministries and their directorates divide the administrative load as in most nations. Two directorates are enough different from Western experience to be worthy of comment. The Directorate of Public Waqfs supervises the management of all Muslim charitable trusts for the maintenance of mosques, orphanages, and other such endowed charitable institutions. A sub-agency, the Zakat, disburses money for charity of all kinds, supervises the religious schools, and decides all questions related to *Sharia,* or the religious laws of Islam. Both agencies discharge the obligation of all good Muslims to give alms, one of the pillars of Islam.

The Directorate of Tribal Affairs under the Minister of the Interior probably has the most headaches. It is their job to try to settle the Bedouin tribes on fixed areas of land and stop their age-old habit of wandering about and raiding each other. They have made no attempt to change the structure of Bedouin life, consisting of families forming clans, which, in turn, form tribes. Each group elects a leader of proven ability. These leaders, in turn, form a council of elders who elect and advise the Sheikh whose leadership and word are law.

Nor is there any attempt on the part of the Syrian government to interfere with tribal customs except in cases of murder and property damage when the civil courts assess payments and prohibit blood feuds. Bedouins coming into settled areas must also leave their rifles

A modern classroom in Damascus.

with the local gendarmerie, much as cowboys had to check in their guns at the old-time western dance halls. The government does provide doctors and schoolteachers and encourages the tribes to settle beside newly drilled deep wells. These wells, however, are not the property of the tribe but are free to any nomad group needing water and must be shared without quarreling.

The Syrian government has also recognized the importance of a basic education for all citizens. It is spending large sums and much effort on training teachers and building schools throughout the country. The old practice of teaching the students to memorize verses of the Koran, where the student who shouted the loudest was rated the best scholar, has given way to a modern curriculum in the best tradition of Arab scholarship. In addition, the teachers sent to the villages are trained to advise in modern methods of farming, pest control, fertilizers, and the raising of livestock and poultry.

Every *Muhaffasite,* or district, is governed by an appointed *Muhaffis,* who is responsible for the schools as well as for the administration and policing of the district. Modern government schools and trained teachers are rapidly supplementing the efforts of the private and religious schools that could reach only a small part of the population.

The Syrian University in Damascus has been expanded to offer courses in the humanities, medicine, education, law, and science. At Aleppo, the Syrian Northern University offers degrees in all types of engineering, and recently has added colleges of medicine, pharmacy, and law. A grant from the Ford Foundation made it possible to establish an experimental farm at Sélemié, near Homs. Staffed originally with American agriculturalists, it got a good start and now plays an important role in the agricultural economy. The students are numbered in the thousands.

Private schools have played and will continue to play an important role in Syrian education. Nearly all of the many religious and foreign schools have been nationalized. In Aleppo the French Marist

Frères maintain a large preparatory school and the Franciscan Order a high school named Terre Sainte. An endowed technical school named after its founder, Georges Salem, provides training in various trades.

A college founded by Americans in 1927, with preparatory schools for both boys and girls, occupies a fine campus on the western rim of the city. It was named Aleppo College. Most of the graduates

A laboratory in the Syrian University of Damascus.

Students at Aleppo College.

go on to the Syrian Universities, the American University of Beirut, or on scholarships to foreign colleges.

Besides having an active concern for general education, Syria has a number of "firsts" to her credit in the Arab world. She was the first Arab country to recognize and protect the General Federation of Trade Unions, which carry on the best traditions of the medieval guilds. Syria was first to start distributing state-owned lands to farmers in an effort to break up land monopolies. Her policy of settling the nomadic tribes has now been adopted by Iraq and Jordan. Also, Syria is the first country in the Arab world to grant women the right to vote in parliamentary elections provided they have an elementary-school education.

In the literary world Syria has not produced any great figures to equal those of the Middle Ages. Her present literary magazines and newspapers are too numerous and too limited in circulation to be effective in shaping policies. Newspapers are either privately owned or are the mouthpieces of political or religious parties and are limited in their influence on national affairs.

Instead, the mass of citizens depend on the government radio-broadcasts, with the news slanted in favor of the party in power at the moment; or they are overwhelmed by powerful Radio Cairo.

Syrian women casting their ballots.

Although the political picture is not too satisfactory and will need time and maturity to resolve its difficulties, the cultural life of the people is expanding rapidly. The airplane has again made the Middle East the crossroads of commerce and culture. Nations vie with each other to send to the Arab states lecturers, musicians, orchestras, ballets, bands, and even basketball teams like the Harlem Globetrotters. As entertainment and propaganda, documentary and instructional films are shown in the villages by the government and other information agencies.

The people are not solely dependent on visiting artists for cultural stimulation. Several chapters of the Archaeological Society of Syria flourish and keep alive a pride in their rich heritage. An international show of paintings is held annually in Damascus at the National Museum. The painters are, for the most part, trained in or follow the French school, and tend to be academic in style. The artists are, however, appreciating and painting the local scene, finding new beauty in the world immediately around them. Eventually, the artists will develop a distinctive Syrian style; some encouraging attempts have been made toward that goal.

In the more practical field of economics Syria has been making progress on her development projects neglected during the union with Egypt. Some few plans for improvement, already under way, have been pushed to completion. The great marshes of the Rhab, northwest of Hama, created by the sluggish movement of the Orontes River and by winter rain drainage from the mountains, have been drained to allow thousands of acres to be reclaimed for farming.

At Maharde on the southern edge of the Rhab, a dam, started in 1962, was built to hold back the flood waters and increase the irrigated acres. Both it and the dam at Rustan on the Orontes River, started in 1961, provide electric power for the increased acreage to the east: the whole region from Homs to Hama.

Construction of a much-needed railroad from the modern port of Latakia to the Jezire in the northeast corner of Syria will enable cotton crops to be carried cheaply to the textile mills at Aleppo and to the port of Latakia.

Another project, financed by West Germany and nearing completion, is a large dam on the Euphrates River at Tapaqa, southeast of Aleppo. The dam diverts water to irrigate nearly three million acres of land and provides cheaper electric power for the northern area.

Many of the ancient canals, tunneled underground to prevent evaporation, have been traced and reopened. It was these canals, wrecked by the Mongols, that had provided water to make the northern Syrian desert bloom in Roman times. Deep-drilled wells have tapped an unexpected source of water far below the rapidly shrinking water table, now nearly exhausted by shallow wells.

Cotton is Syria's most important single export, earning more than two hundred million Syrian pounds. But crops of the lowly lentils, oats, chick-peas, broad beans, and vetch together add more than three hundred fifty million pounds to Syria's economy each year. Wheat and barley, once major exports, are now consumed locally.

The Cotton Control Board has developed a cross between Ameri-

The huge dam on the Euphrates River, now nearing completion, will restore the irrigation system of northern Syria.

can and Egyptian long-staple cotton. Named "Palmyra," it promises a heavy yield of superior cotton for export mainly to Russia. Cotton gins have been put under state control, along with the monopolistic textile industry. Flour mills have also been nationalized.

The ministry of agriculture has set December 24 as a Tree Festival to encourage tree planting, much like Arbor Day in America. Thousands of fruit trees are distributed free to the farmers each year. Citrus fruit and orange trees are being planted along the narrow coastal plain from Latakia south to Tartous. Along the inner belt from Damascus to Aleppo the pistachio orchards are being doubled and thousands of olive trees planted to replace those lost in the great freeze of 1950, when even nine-hundred-year-old trees died. The reforestation program that had lagged for years is now being pushed

A textile factory near Damascus—one of many in Syria.

ahead vigorously. Goats are prohibited in all areas where their vandalism might damage the young trees.

Syria has had a stormy political voyage after separating from Egypt in 1961. It is easier to control crops than it is to control politicians. Transition cabinets and ministries struggled to improve economic conditions and to resolve political differences. Their efforts were hampered in the former by years of lean harvests, and in the latter by a succession of military *coups d'état*. Political leaders rose and fell. A hard core of owners holding large tracts of land resisted attempts to create a class of small independent farmers.

TOMORROW

Syria and her sister Arab nations have a better chance of success than, for instance, do the new nations of central Africa. A number of factors contribute to their advantage in this troubled world. Sociologists have developed a formula for predicting the future of a nation:

$$L + H + RPO + X = \text{The Future.}$$

Location plus History plus Resources, People, and Organization, plus the unknown factor X gives us a chance to peer into the crystal ball, through which we may glimpse the Future.

Syria has always occupied a strategic *location* at the crossroads of trade between East and West. On the whole she enjoys a climate favorable for year-round travel and settlement. Although the summers can be uncomfortably hot, the winters do not send paralyzing snowstorms to block highways. On the other hand easy travel implies the lack of natural barriers that have left and still leave Syria open to easy invasion. The desert is no longer the deterrent it once was, in this age of plane and tank. That is why peace with Israel is so important.

In the field of *history,* Syria is unusually rich. Her heritage is a roll call of many ancient civilizations which have left her their cultures. This heritage of varied ideas will be better appreciated as education becomes more general. The strength of this heritage can, however, be weakened if minority groups let their petty differences interfere with their concern for national progress.

In *resources,* Syria is more fortunate than many of the other Arab countries in that she can eventually absorb and feed three times her present population. Water resources are being expanded and used to better advantage in reclaiming idle lands. Oil discovered in the Jezire, promising three million tons or more a year, will give Syria the extra revenue to carry out many projects now hampered by lack of funds.

The Syrian *people* are a healthy stock with a good birth rate. Their diet is sufficiently well-balanced to sustain sound bodies and gleaming teeth. Hospitals and sanitariums carry on a vigorous battle against infant diseases, tuberculosis, malaria, and bilharziasis. Inflamed eyes and blindness from the ever-blowing desert dust are of primary concern. Government doctors are attacking the problems with mobile medical units. The Arab Muslim, washing five times a day before devotions, is a cleanly person and a healthy citizen.

On the other hand, *organizations* have not prospered in Syria. Often Ottoman suspicion of any group-gathering led to suppression and often prison. Nor were the French authorities, under the mandate, any more lenient. Since independence, athletic clubs have been encouraged, sports events given government sponsorship, and international service clubs granted charters. But the Arab's natural tendency to individualism hampers his participation in organizations through which he might learn to ignore party differences and to appreciate the added strength of united effort.

The most encouraging sign of progress is the new activity of Syrian women. More and more women are going to work in offices, stores, and factories. Many affluent women are giving their time and effort in public service. They serve in the Red Crescent, Eastern branch of the International Red Cross, and are organizing and managing schools, orphanages, hospitals, and homes for delinquent children. Moreover they are taking an interest in national affairs where their natural sense of realism and practicality should do much to stabilize politics.

Balanced against these encouraging signs of progress is an almost equal number of upsetting political changes that Syria has experienced during the last twenty years. These unfortunate events culminated in the humiliating excursion into Jordan in 1970. Syria went to the support of the Palestinians fighting against King Hussein but the Palestinians were defeated and the Syrian troops were routed back across the border. This unhappy event brought to a close the long regime of the Ba'athist Party, whose socialist policies were now unpopular.

On November 13, 1970, General Hafiz Al-Assad easily took over the reins of government. He is a handsome six-footer in uniform who also likes to dress in sloppy mufti. The people welcomed him as one of themselves. He has rescinded many of the restrictions so unpopular with peasant and businessman alike. An increased amount of consumer goods from eastern Europe is available in the shops. It is wryly amusing that the buyer unfamiliar with the brands is told the product is "Americanish" or of the best quality. Assad has managed to get help from the Russians without having to give too much in return. He takes a hard line with Israel; after all, it is a squatter on the Golan Heights only twenty miles from Damascus. Tourists are welcomed—even Americans, who had been in disfavor because the United States was blamed for the Israeli use of American-made planes as early as the Suez crisis of 1956.

On March 12, 1971 the Syrians went to the polls and voted to make Assad president for a six-year term. This reflected a disavowal of the Ba'ath dictatorship and a faith in the army as being more moderate, flexible, and aware of the outside world. Tentative advances have been made to the West which in time should help to stabilize policies in the Middle East.

Of course X, the unknown factor, remains. Will better education create better opportunities for her citizens? Can Syria achieve peace? Can she resist the conflicting appeals of power politics and the abrasions of her neighbors' ambitions? Will religion become an active, creative force instead of the resigned philosophy of *In'shallah* (If God is willing)? Only time, resolution, and faith will tell the story.

INDEX